LLEWE

2 0

Witches'
Spell-A-Day
Almanac

Holidays & Lore
Spells, Rituals & Meditations

© 2020 Llewellyn Worldwide Ltd.
Cover design by the Llewellyn Art Department
Interior art © 2018 Laura Tempest Zakroff: pages 9, 29,
47, 67, 87, 109, 131, 153, 173, 193, 213, 231
Spell icons throughout © 2011 Sherrie Thai

You can order Llewellyn books and annuals from *New Worlds*,
Llewellyn's catalog. To request a free copy of the catalog, call toll-free
1-877-NEW WRLD or visit our website at www.llewellyn.com.

ISBN: 978-0-7387-5491-8

Llewellyn is a registered trademark of Llewellyn Worldwide Ltd.
2143 Wooddale Drive
Woodbury, MN 55125

Printed in the United States of America

Contents

A Note on Magic and Spells

The spells in the *Witches' Spell-A-Day Almanac* evoke everyday magic designed to improve our lives and homes. You needn't be an expert on magic to follow these simple rites and spells; as you will see if you use these spells throughout the year, magic, once mastered, is easy to perform. The only advanced technique required of you is the art of visualization.

Visualization is an act of controlled imagination. If you can call up in your mind a picture of your best friend's face or a flag flapping in the breeze, you can visualize. In magic, visualizations are used to direct and control magical energies. Basically the spellcaster creates a visual image of the spell's desired goal, whether it be perfect health, a safe house, or a protected pet.

Visualization is the basis of all good spells, and as such it is a tool that should be properly used. Visualization must be real in the mind of the spellcaster so it allows him or her to raise, concentrate, and send forth energy to accomplish the spell.

Perhaps when visualizing you'll find that you're doing everything right, but you don't feel anything. This is common, for we haven't been trained to acknowledge—let alone utilize—our magical abilities. Keep practicing, however, for your spells can "take" even if you're not the most experienced natural magician.

You will notice also that many spells in this collection have a some-what "light" tone. They are seemingly fun and frivolous, filled with rhyme and colloquial speech. This is not to diminish the seriousness of the purpose, but rather to create a relaxed atmosphere for the practitio-ner. Lightness of spirit helps focus energy; rhyme and common language help the spellcaster remember the words and train the mind where it is needed. The intent of this magic is indeed very serious at times, and magic is never to be trifled with.

Even when your spells are effective, magic won't usually sparkle before your very eyes. The test of magic's success is time, not immediate eye-popping results. But you can feel magic's energy for yourself by rubbing your palms together briskly for ten seconds, then holding them a few inches apart. Sense the energy passing through them, the warm tingle in your palms. This is the power raised and used in magic. It comes from within and is perfectly natural.

Among the features of the *Witches' Spell-A-Day Almanac* are an easy-to-use "book of days" format; new spells specifically tailored for each day of the year (and its particular magical, astrological, and historical energies); and additional tips and lore for various days throughout the year—including color correspondences based on planetary influences, obscure and forgotten holidays and festivals, and an incense of the day to help you waft magical energies from the ether into your space. Moon signs, phases, and voids are also included to help you find the perfect time for your rituals and spells. (All times in this book are Eastern Standard Time or Eastern Daylight Time.)

Enjoy your days, and have a magical year!

Spell-A-Day Icons

 New Moon

 Meditation, Divination

 Full Moon

 Money, Prosperity

 Abundance

 Protection

 Altar

 Relationship

 Balance

 Success

 Clearing, Cleaning

 Travel, Communication

 Garden

 Air Element

 Grab Bag

 Earth Element

 Health, Healing

 Fire Element

 Home

 Spirit Element

 Heart, Love

Water Element

Spells at a Glance by Date and Category*

	Health, Healing	Protection	Success	Heart, Love	Clearing, Cleaning	Home	Meditation, Divination
Jan.	8, 9, 16	3, 25	4, 30, 31	29	17		1, 10, 12, 18
Feb.		10, 22	12	14, 15, 24	1, 7, 9, 28	5	2
March	21, 29, 31	23	16, 30	1, 14	2, 7, 15		12, 25
April	23		12, 21		20, 25, 27, 30	24	3, 13
May	14	18, 27		1, 12, 22	24	9, 17	28, 30
June	6, 13	14, 25	12	7, 22	1, 2	9, 29	
July	11, 18, 27	25, 31	8	13	29	28	3
Aug.	5	14	21, 23	27, 29	9, 25, 31	6	11, 26
Sept.	1, 21	5	4, 9, 17, 29	8, 10, 14	2, 16, 23, 25	7, 28	13
Oct.	5	4	15	8	9, 17, 25, 30	5, 8	2, 3, 11, 16, 19, 21, 23, 29
Nov.	18, 20	23, 30		14, 16	11	28	2, 6, 7
Dec.	6, 8, 9, 27	5, 7, 17, 23	11, 26		3, 14, 31	19, 21	

*List is not comprehensive.

2021

Year of Spells

January

Happy New Year! The calendar year has begun and even though we may be in the depths of winter (in the Northern Hemisphere) or the height of summer (in the Southern Hemisphere), we stand at the threshold of fifty-two weeks filled with promise. Legend has it that this month is named to honor the Roman god Janus, a god of new beginnings and doorways, but it is also associated with Juno, the primary goddess of the Roman pantheon. Juno was said to be the protectress of the Roman Empire, and Janus (whose twin faces look to both the past and the future simultaneously) encourages new endeavors, transitions, and change in all forms. Since this month marks the beginning of the whole year, we can plant the seeds for long-term goals at this time, carefully plotting the course of our future success.

In the United States, there are three important holidays occurring in January: New Year's Day, Martin Luther King Jr. Day, and Inauguration Day. Each of these days exemplifies powerful change and transition. The dawn of a new year heralds a fresh start, and whether snow-covered or bathed in summer heat, January offers renewed possibilities for all.

Michael Furie

January 1
Friday

3rd ♌

Color of the Day: Rose
Incense of the Day: Vanilla

New Year's Day – Kwanzaa ends

Coins of Blessing Divination Spell

For this spell you will need a deck of tarot cards and thirteen coins.

Ground and center. Draw a tarot card of your choice that represents your success, and place it in the center of your working area as a "manifestation guide" for your spell.

Shuffle your cards while focusing on the year ahead. Deal out twelve cards, face down, in a clockwise circle around the central card, naming each as a month.

Take the coins in your hands and make a heartfelt prayer for your success. Imagine breathing this prayer into the coins. Hold them as you turn over each card, reflecting on its meaning. If you find a "negative" card, place a coin upon it (heads-up) as a transformative blessing and say:

In the month of (name of month), a challenge is struck,

But a coin of blessing turns my luck.

Read the cards to show the year's journey toward success. Spend the coins on yourself.

Storm Faerywolf

January 2
Saturday

3rd ♌

☽ v/c 5:00 pm
☽ → ♍ 8:13 pm

Color of the Day: Indigo
Incense of the Day: Ivy

A Transformation Spell

Winter is a time for transformation. The earth quietly begins to change too—bulbs begin to send up growth and seeds drowse before they stir with life as spring nears. It's also a good time to cast a spell to bring about a positive transformation in your life.

For this spell you'll need colored pencils, a plain sheet of white paper, an envelope, and a pinch of soil. (Potting soil will do.) Select the colored pencils of your choice, then write down what it is you wish to transform. It could be a new home, a different job, etc. Draw a picture of it too. Fold the paper and put it in the envelope with a bit of soil. Seal the envelope and hide it. Keep it until Imbolc. At Imbolc, either throw away the envelope and its contents or bury it. The transformation should now begin to take place.

James Kambos

January 3
Sunday

3rd ♏

Color of the Day: Amber
Incense of the Day: Heliotrope

Warning Bell Bracelet

Now is the perfect time to raid the craft store for discounted holiday items, one of which is jingle bells. These are available in many colors and sizes. For this protection amulet, you'll need three small jingle bells (about the size of a large berry) in the color of your choice, along with a piece of black ribbon that can be tied around your wrist or ankle.

Gather the bells and ribbon in a quiet spot where you won't be disturbed. Hold one bell in your hand and say:

This one protects me.

String it onto the ribbon.
Hold the second bell in your hand and say:

This one sends a warning.

String it onto the ribbon.
Hold the last bell and say:

This one defends me.

String it onto the ribbon.
Tie the ribbon securely around your wrist or ankle. When you feel negative energy approaching, subtly shake the bells to send out protective, defensive vibrations all around you.

Kate Freuler

January 4
Monday

3rd ♏

☽ v/c 4:34 pm

Color of the Day: White
Incense of the Day: Hyssop

Appreciation Spell

The moon is in organized but eager Virgo today, which means it is a great day to make sure you are getting the attention and support you deserve. If you feel like you are under-appreciated in any area of your life, cast this spell and watch the power of Virgo make it right.

Place the Three of Pentacles (Coins) card from any tarot deck under a firesafe dish or candleholder and then affix a purple candle to the dish/holder. Take three deep breaths, light the candle, and say:

Virgo Moon and Three of Coin,

Purple light, your power join!

Show them my worth and all I do.

Give the oblivious a freaking clue!

Allow the candle to burn out on its own, then discard any remaining wax and put the card back in the deck.

Devin Hunter

January 5
Tuesday

3rd ♏

☽ → ♎ 12:42 am

Color of the Day: Gray
Incense of the Day: Geranium

Just Desserts Abundance Spell

Today is National Whipped Cream Day in the United States. Cream (and butter) has long had otherworldly and magical associations, particularly for transformation, since cream can take so many forms. This correspondence is ideal for ensuring that even in the barren time of winter, there shall still be abundance in our lives. For this simple spell, all that is needed is a carton of heavy whipping cream, a mixing bowl, your preferred sweetener, a hand mixer, and your favorite dessert.

Pour the cream in the bowl and add the sweetener. Hold both hands over the bowl and charge the cream with the intention that any who partake of it shall enjoy abundance. Whip the cream with the mixer until it has thickened nicely, then add a big spoonful of it to your dessert. Eat the dessert and take into yourself the magic of abundance. Share with whomever you choose.

Michael Furie

January 6
Wednesday

3rd ♎

4th Quarter 4:37 am

Color of the Day: Brown
Incense of the Day: Honeysuckle

Repair Miscommunication

When you find yourself in a difficult situation caused by miscommunication, try this spell.

Dress a yellow or white candle with rosemary essential oil, then safely light it. You can also burn rosemary incense alongside your candle. Visualize the issue being resolved, and take action to repair the situation in whatever way you can.

Chant the following words three times—as you dress the candle with oil (or light the incense), as you light the candle, and one more time after lighting it:

To clear the air,

To understand,

I/We really need a helping hand.

State your intent. Let the candle burn out and then discard it.

Ember Grant

January 7
Thursday

4th ♎

☽ v/c 12:55 am

☽ → ♏ 3:53 am

Color of the Day: Green
Incense of the Day: Clove

Fly Like an Arrow

One morning as I stood outside sipping my coffee, a squadron of Canada geese flew over my head. They were honking loudly and were close enough that I could actually hear their wings flapping. It was a thrilling experience.

I began pondering the question "Are you in the lead or part of the team?" Sometimes it's good to be in the lead, and other times it's good to be part of the pack.

Use this spell to help you fly confidently in the direction that supports the achievement of your goals, dreams, and desires.

Gather seven stones. Hold them in your dominant hand. Focus on the directions of north, east, south, and west. On a flat surface, place your stones in a V formation. Say:

As the geese fly away,

These stones will help me find my way.

Whether I go north, south,
east, or west,

These stones will help me do my best.

Seal the spell by tossing your stones upon the earth.

Najah Lightfoot

Notes:

January 8
Friday

4th ♏

☽ v/c 8:59 pm

Color of the Day: Rose
Incense of the Day: Orchid

Affirmation for Peace

We live in a chaotic world, constantly bombarded by bad news, too many demands on our time and energy, and lots of electronic gizmos that distract us from the quiet blessings around us. It can be hard to find peace. From time to time, it helps to take a moment to simply let yourself stop and take a breath.

Try doing this affirmation for a moment or two every day and see if it helps. If you have time, you can sit in front of a candle or look out a window. But you can always just find a quiet place (bathrooms work!) and close your eyes for just a minute. Breathe in and out slowly, place your hands on your core (over your belly), and say:

> *I am a child of the Goddess and*
> *I am surrounded by her love.*
> *I am calm and at peace.*

> Deborah Blake

January 9
Saturday

4th ♏

☽ → ♐ 6:15 am

Color of the Day: Blue
Incense of the Day: Patchouli

Healing Beads

January is a good time to cast spells for the coming year. This one focuses on health and healing. For this spell you will need three beads. If possible, choose healing stones such as aventurine, chrysoprase, and malachite. If you can't find those, use three different shades of green glass.

Name each of the three beads for an aspect of health you want, such as body, mind, and spirit or heart, lungs, and liver. Hold each bead in your hand and concentrate on its meaning. Then string them together. You can make them into something specific (like a necklace, bracelet, or key chain) or just a knotted loop.

Hold the whole piece in your hand and focus on your overall health for the year ahead. You can leave the beads in a safe place where you spend a lot of time, such as your bedroom, or you can carry them with you to support your health.

> Elizabeth Barrette

January 10
Sunday

4♄ ♐
☽ v/c 1:29 pm

Color of the Day: Yellow
Incense of the Day: Frankincense

Save the Eagles Day

Today is Save the Eagles Day. Although in recent years bald eagles have been increasing in number, other species are still threatened. Further, some legislators have threatened to remove the protected status of some species still in need of it.

Today, spend a few moments to connect with the spirit of the eagle. Take a comfortable seat, outside in the fresh air if possible, and center yourself. Close your eyes and enter a meditative trance state. Visualize that your arms have become feathered. Pay attention to how they feel in the air around you. Notice how your vision has changed. Note how your eagle vision is different from your ordinary human vision. How has your perspective on the world changed? Ask the spirit of the eagle what you can do to help it. After sitting with this experience for a few moments, slowly bring yourself back to ordinary reality and journal about your experience.

Blake Octavian Blair

 # January 11
Monday

4♄ ♐
☽ → ♑ 8:30 am

Color of the Day: Lavender
Incense of the Day: Neroli

First Snow Spell

The first snow of the year is enchanting! When sparkly snowflakes cover the natural landscape, there is a sense of renewal and childlike innocence. Gathering snow from the first snowfall of the year is a wonderful way to cleanse and purify your crystals. If you cannot collect the first snow, do not despair: this spell can be used with snow during the entire winter season. If it doesn't snow where you live, gather raindrops in a clear glass container during the first full moon of the year (which will be on January 28, 2021).

After you collect the snow, place it in a bowl with the items you want to cleanse. Make sure your crystals will not be damaged by the water or the cold temperature. The most important ingredient in any spell is you and your intention. Repeat these words as you focus your powerful magickal intention on cleansing and purifying your crystals with the snow:

> *Purify and cleanse these crystals*
> *for me with this magickal snow*
> *(rainwater). Blessed be!*

Sapphire Moonbeam

January 12
Tuesday

4th ♑

Color of the Day: Maroon
Incense of the Day: Cinnamon

Ask for Guidance

Create time to ask for guidance from your higher self today. Set aside ten to twenty minutes in a safe and private space. Sit with your hands on your thighs and breathe deeply. Inhale to a count of four and exhale to a count of six. A longer exhale stimulates the vagus nerve, slows the heart rate, and creates calm.

Exhale and envision stress leaving your body, blowing a black cloud out and away from you. Inhale, welcoming fresh oxygen and bringing vitality into the body.

After about thirty breaths, or when you notice the calming of your heart rate, ask for guidance from your higher self:

*Guide me to know which way
to go in the year ahead, for
my own highest purpose.*

Breathe another thirty breaths, inhaling for four counts and exhaling for six. Listen for the whispers of your own higher truth and watch for a vision of what is to come.

Dallas Jennifer Cobb

January 13
Wednesday

4th ♑
New Moon 12:00 am
☽ v/c 2:22 am
☽ → ♒ 11:44 am

Color of the Day: White
Incense of the Day: Lilac

Step-by-Step New Moon Spell

Did you make a New Year's resolution this year? Many people just don't seem to be able to keep their promises, no matter how good their intentions. Usually it's because their resolution was a bit too drastic. A great solution is to set smaller goals over the course of the entire year that add up to big changes come December. The new moon is an ideal time to set intentions. As the moon grows in the sky, so does your motivation!

Think about what big change you want to make by the end of the year, and break it into twelve stages. At each new moon this year, you will set your intention to take the next step toward success.

Write your intention for this first month on a slip of paper. Safely light a white candle and read it aloud within your personal sacred space. Keep the paper where you can read it every day and monitor your progress. When

the next new moon arrives, it is time to move on to the next phase of your goal! Be sure to extinguish the candle.

Thorn Mooney

NOTES:

January 14
Thursday

1st ♒

☽ v/c 4:28 am

Color of the Day: Turquoise
Incense of the Day: Apricot

Invocation for Peace

Winter can be a difficult time, when the days are short and the nights are long, and light and warmth are in short supply. But there is a benefit to these things as well. The world is quieter and slower, and if you so desire, you can tap into this natural lull in energy to find that quiet inside yourself.

First thing in the morning, or at some time in the evening before you go to bed, take a minute to say this simple invocation for peace. (You can do this on any day during the winter season.) If you want, you can light a candle first, making sure it is some-place safe so you can sit without worry as it burns down.

> Quiet of winter,
>
> Calm of winter,
>
> Be within me, as you are without.
>
> Bring me peace.
>
> So mote it be.

Deborah Blake

 # January 15
Friday

1st ♒︎

☽ → ♓︎ 5:17 pm

Color of the Day: Coral
Incense of the Day: Rose

Awaken the Spirit of an Altar

An altar is a space equipped with symbols and tools devoted to particular aspects of magic or spirituality, whether deity, spirit, or philosophy. Over time, altars become attuned to the energies that are worked with them. When erecting an altar, we should ideally be in tune with our creative process to allow divine inspiration to guide us. This is a simple spell to help you align with that inspiration to further empower and awaken your altar space.

You will need a small piece of paper and a pen. Ground and center. Concentrate on the purpose of your altar. On the paper, draw a pentagram, and in the center of it, draw an open eye. Chant over it three times:

Awaken unto life and be

A place to reach between the worlds.

Take a deep breath of power and then exhale over the paper, "seeing" the symbols shine. Hide the paper somewhere on your new altar.

Storm Faerywolf

January 16
Saturday

1st ♓︎

Color of the Day: Gray
Incense of the Day: Sage

Fresh Footbath Forward

Take a thrice-wise footbath today to recharge your endurance and inner warmth for the long, cold days ahead. As you assemble the following ingredients, imagine the gestation and manifestations of spring. While soaking your feet, visualize the path ahead of you as glowing and golden. Be forewarned that this spell will stain your skin and towels yellow. You are about to be very lucky for a few days, and this fortune will transfer but not wash away easily, so make it count!

Combine the following ingredients in a large foot tub and soak your feet for thirty minutes. Repeat this spell *three times* today for the very best results, and a golden path will lay itself before your feet.

- 4 tablespoons turmeric powder
- 4 tablespoons Hawaiian black salt
- 1 cup potato flakes
- 1 teaspoon mustard powder
- 1 teaspoon ginger
- 2 tablespoons rice vinegar
- 2 gallons very warm water

Estha McNevin

January 17
Sunday

1st ♓

☽ v/c 10:44 pm

Color of the Day: Orange
Incense of the Day: Hyacinth

Mental/Emotional Clarity Spell

With the Moon in Pisces and Mercury in Aquarius, this is the perfect time to do workings that can help bring clarity to the emotional and mental aspects of our lives. Perform this spell to lift the fog and bring peace to these areas so you can focus on what is truly important at this time.

In a teacup, combine one tablespoon each of dried lavender flower, dried chamomile flower, and fresh ginger root. Then fill the cup three-quarters of the way with hot water. Cover and steep for three minutes, strain, and then add the fresh juice of one whole orange. Stir clockwise nine times and say:

Break the mold and seal the crack,

Clear the way; bring vision back.

What would block me now be gone,

Dark to light just like the dawn.

Drink the tea and then spin counterclockwise three times before saying:

And so it is.

Devin Hunter

January 18
Monday

1st ♓

☽ → ♈ 2:07 am

Color of the Day: Ivory
Incense of the Day: Clary sage

Martin Luther King Jr. Day

Pendulum Divination

I purchased my pendulum many years ago at a craft fair. I chose it solely on the basis of the color of the stone. Sadly, I put it aside and it sat in a drawer, forgotten for almost a decade.

After taking a class on crystals and pendulums a few years ago, I put into practice the simple instructions and was amazed at the results. So far I have not gotten beyond "yes" and "no" questions. There is no guarantee of any answer. For some, pendulums are the only magic they employ. For others, like me, a pendulum is just one of the many tools in their bag. Pendulums can be enlightening yet very tricky and complicated. As with any tool, do not take their power lightly. Look for a workshop if you wish to become adept at the practice. Invoke:

As I embark on a journey and
seek the perfect pendulum for my
practice, please guide my hand.
Assist me in not rushing into a faulty
relationship with this prophetic tool.
I will know it by the vibration.

Emyme

January 19

Tuesday

1st ♈

☉ → ♒ 3:40 pm

Color of the Day: Black
Incense of the Day: Ylang-ylang

Birdseed Travel Spell

Ready for a vacation but unsure how you're going to make it happen? Put in a request with the most frequent flyers of all: the birds. As creatures of the air element, birds cover large distances, representing travel, communication, and movement. All you need for this spell is a handful of birdseed and a quiet outdoor place where you know many birds live.

Place the seeds on the ground, using them to carefully spell out the name of the destination you want to travel to. Visualize your trip as if you're already experiencing it, exactly as you wish it to be. What does it sound like? Is it sunny? Is there water? Who is with you?

Listen for a moment to the birds singing, acknowledging their presence. Say:

Feather and flight, soaring birds,

Take my wishes to the sky.

To manifest my travel goals,

My dreams grow wings and fly.

Let the birds eat the seed and carry your wishes far and wide into the air.
Kate Freuler

NOTES:

January 20
Wednesday

1st ♈

☽ v/c 3:29 am

☽ → ♉ 1:56 pm

2nd Quarter 4:02 pm

Color of the Day: Topaz
Incense of the Day: Marjoram

Inauguration Day

Spell for Spiritual Alignment

At times we may feel disconnected from our path, as if there's some sort of cosmic signal interference disrupting our ability to receive messages from spirit. When this happens, a spell to unblock energy and revitalize our connections is needed.

You will need a white candle and a holder, a little olive oil, and some matches. Anoint the candle from the top down, mentally charging it with the intention that it will help you restore inner balance. Place the candle in its holder and light it. As the flame ignites, visualize a beam of white light descending from the sky, pouring energy into your body, passing through your chakras, and moving down into the earth. As the light passes through you, envision it sweeping away any psychic blockages from your system, releasing them into the earth to be recycled, and repeat:

Cosmic light, make it right.

Return my power, restore my might.

When you feel cleansed, end the visualization and extinguish the candle.

Michael Furie

NOTES:

January 21
Thursday

2nd ♉

Color of the Day: Purple
Incense of the Day: Jasmine

Patience Spell

Based on the popular Serenity Prayer, this spell draws on the characteristics of the four elements to help you foster patience and balance in difficult situations.

Place a clear quartz point or cluster in a clear jar or glass bowl and fill it with water. Light a floating candle on the water (or beside the jar or bowl). This represents the four elements we need for life; visualize them giving you strength. Chant this as you gaze upon them:

*By water I'm balanced to
go with the flow,*

*While earth keeps me grounded
and stable to grow.*

Air gives me insight so I understand;

*With the courage of fire,
I change what I can.*

Allow the candle to burn out, then discard it. Pour the water outside (or on a plant) as an offering. Carry the stone with you or keep it in a place where you can see it.

Ember Grant

 January 22
Friday

2nd ♉

☽ v/c 4:28 pm

Color of the Day: White
Incense of the Day: Cypress

Get Rid of the Blues Spell

In the winter, mild depression can be a problem. This spell can help you beat the blues. Perform it during the day.

You'll need three white votive candles. Cover an altar or a table with a white cloth. Place the candles on the altar, but don't light them yet. Lower the blinds, close the drapes, and turn off the lights. Now say:

Darkness, you know me well,

*But you're not strong
enough for this spell.*

Blues and sadness take flight.

Joy return with this light!

Now safely light each candle. As you light them, visualize your blues diminishing. Then open the drapes, raise the blinds, and turn on all the lights. Your mood should feel lighter. Make a cup of tea and relax. End the spell by snuffing out all the candles. When they've cooled, throw them away.

James Kambos

 # January 23
Saturday

2nd ♉

☽ → ♊ 2:43 am

Color of the Day: Indigo
Incense of the Day: Rue

handwritten Magic

Much magic relies on writing. We write spells and books. We inscribe words or names on stones, candles, wands, and other magical tools. We create magical alphabets such as runes and ogham. These work better when handwritten than when typed or printed out.

Today is National Handwriting Day, so take some time to practice the magic of handwriting. For this exercise you'll need a pen. A ballpoint pen will do, a fountain pen is better, and a dip nib is best of all. (Most magical inks are designed to work only with dip nibs.) You'll also need a nice piece of paper, like parchment or linen, but one with not too much texture. Finally, you'll need a ribbon.

Write the complete alphabet on the paper, forming each letter with intent. In English, "The quick brown fox jumps over the lazy dog" uses every letter once. Choose a different writing system if you like. Roll up the page and tie it with the ribbon. Keep the scroll on your altar so the gods know your handwriting.

Elizabeth Barrette

 # January 24
Sunday

2nd ♊

Color of the Day: Gold
Incense of the Day: Marigold

Sun Day, Sun Day!

The sun is a solar deity, honored since the beginning of human time. It's 93 million miles away, yet its presence is undeniably felt and depended upon. We mark our days and years by the sun, some people even choosing to call their birthdays "solar returns." Countless civilizations have had rituals, rites, and beliefs that embody and honor the sun. The sun is self-sufficient and fiercely independent. Its light brightens the darkest corners and chases shadows away.

Today, in honor of the sun, anoint a yellow candle with olive oil and sprinkle it with gold glitter. Place the candle in a fireproof holder and light it.

Gaze into the candle flame and reflect upon the powerful light of the sun. Think about how the sun's light shines into and upon the darkness of space, illuminating our world with grace.

Allow your candle to burn down safely or snuff out the flame.

Najah Lightfoot

January 25
Monday

2nd ♊

☽ v/c 2:17 am

☽ → ♋ 1:52 pm

Color of the Day: Gray
Incense of the Day: Lily

Protect Your Sacred Space

Today is A Room of One's Own Day, in honor of Virginia Woolf's birthday and her famous essay. It is observed by individuals taking time to honor their personal space in which they have the freedom to pray, study, and recharge. We often do our best studying in private spaces where we feel protected. Today, let's work some simple magic that honors and protects our private sacred space. Take a clear quartz crystal (which also resonates with the energies of Monday), hold it up to your third eye, and recite:

My sacred space, I do declare,

A place for study,
rejuvenation, and prayer.

By power of quartz,

May my intentions be crystal clear.

Corporeal and ethereal, only
spirits of benefit may enter here.

Place the quartz near the entrance of your room.

Blake Octavian Blair

January 26
Tuesday

2nd ♋

Color of the Day: Scarlet
Incense of the Day: Basil

Reconnect with Your Power

The first month of the year is a good time to reconnect with your inner power. Collect the essence of a cedar or evergreen tree to connect with the strong purification and grounding energies. (You can substitute materials from any tree that you connect with on a deep level.) Add some pieces of cedar wood, sprigs from the tree branch, and/or a few pine cones to your altar space. If you gather these items from a tree in nature, ask for permission from the tree. Be sure to leave a small offering (such as a flower petal, seed, or natural stone—something that is derived from nature) at the base of the tree in gratitude. Place the items on your altar and chant these words:

I ask for the wisdom and strength
from this tree to be imparted onto me.
Purify my aura and spirit in this hour,
reconnect me with my inner power.

Repeat these words and use this spell as many times as necessary until you feel connected to the strength and magick of your inner power.

Sapphire Moonbeam

January 27
Wednesday

2nd ♋

☽ v/c 12:55 pm

☽ → ♌ 9:54 pm

Color of the Day: Yellow
Incense of the Day: Lavender

Invoke the Sun

Winter often seems to go on forever, and even if you live in a place that doesn't get ice or snow, it can feel dreary and dark. But even though the days are short now and spring seems a long way off, the power of the sun is growing steadily. To bolster your spirits and brighten the day, make a point of greeting the sun and invoking its energy into your life at this time. This is most effective at sunrise, but you can do it whenever you can see the sun in the sky.

Stand outside, if possible, and raise your arms toward the sky, positioning the sun between your open hands. Say:

Sunna, Apollo, Ra,

Amaterasu, Anyanwu,

By the right eye of Horus

And the chariot of Helios,

I invoke the power of the sun.

I am energized by your rays.

I take comfort in your warmth

And carry your light with me in darkness.

So mote it be.

Thorn Mooney

Notes:

☽ January 28
Thursday

2nd ♌

🌕 Full Moon 2:16 pm

Color of the Day: Crimson
Incense of the Day: Nutmeg

howl at the Moon

One of the traditional names for the full moon that falls in January is the Wolf Moon. It is said that name comes from the fact that wolves howl more in January. (It is also called the Cold Moon, for obvious reasons.) Wolves howl to communicate with each other and to express emotion. Ironically, many of us tend to withdraw during the colder winter months, when it may be harder to get out and be with others, so this might be a good time to put a little extra effort into reaching out. You can try actually howling at the moon, or if that doesn't suit you, try singing or chanting. Whichever way you do it, try putting whatever you are feeling into your howl or song. Channel your inner wolf and send your howl out to the moon or to your pack, wherever they are.

Deborah Blake

♡ January 29
Friday

3rd ♌

☽ v/c 8:53 pm

Color of the Day: Purple
Incense of the Day: Yarrow

Freya's Friday Feast

Friday gets its name from Freya, the Norse goddess of love, sex, lust, beauty, sorcery, and fertility. Today is a great day for a love spell. It is said that food is the quickest way to someone's heart, so plan a feast and invite the person of your fancy.

Foods associated with love and lust include strawberries, figs, and honey; oysters, garlic, and asparagus; and bananas, chocolate, and almonds. Each possesses different nutrients and minerals that stimulate fertility, arousal, or receptivity.

Set the table with rose-scented candles and a vase of lavender-colored roses, which are associated with enchantment, love at first sight, and wonder.

When your companion arrives, invoke Freya's blessing that you may feast together, sharing the energy of love, lust, enchantment, and beauty. Say:

I made this feast especially for you.
It's inspired by the Norse goddess
Freya, goddess of love and beauty.
With her spirit, I toast you.

Dallas Jennifer Cobb

January 30
Saturday

3rd ♌

☽ → ♍ 3:02 am

Color of the Day: Blue
Incense of the Day: Magnolia

Lucky Number

Do you know your lucky or special number? Numbers hold potent magic. There are numbers that are generally considered lucky or unlucky—thirteen, for example. However, we all have a number that has special meaning just for us. Look for a number that appears under unusual circumstances or a number that shows up repetitively in your life. The first time it occurs, or the first time you realize that THIS is YOUR number, there is often a strong physical reaction, like energy passing through you. It leaves no room for doubt that this number will follow you through life and aid you, much like a guardian angel or your spirit animal.

Forty or seven, thirteen or eleven—our lucky numbers make themselves known by appearing in our lives daily. With every sighting, offer a word or two of gratitude.

Emyme

January 31
Sunday

3rd ♍

Color of the Day: Yellow
Incense of the Day: Almond

Pointer Finger Magick

What a witch can't do with a flick of their fingers I've yet to discover. In fact, casting magick for opportunity and luck is one of the best ways to spread good karma while feeling awfully witchy with the ol' crooked finger. Pointing out the good things in your day adds to their aura of power. I like to make it a fun game of "where's the witch's joyful pleasure?"

Throughout the day, use your pointer finger to charge, bless, and otherwise designate objects as auspicious. Feel the intended energy and forcefully project it forward. Cast luck on a fountain you admire, or cast love on an elevator button. Fill a parking meter for the day to share pointed blessings of wealth, or enchant any other object you'd like. As the energy of the sun wanes, make your final blessed castings and seek to dream of all the luck and opportunities yet to come to you. Try to point them out even in your dreams.

Estha McNevin

February

The word *February* is based on the Latin *februa* and refers to the Roman festival of purification of the same name. This festival later became integrated with February's infamous Lupercalia. Since ancient times, February has been observed as a month of cleansing, cleaning, purification, and preparation for the warm months ahead. We see the Celtic Imbolg (Candlemas) celebrated in February to perpetuate the summoning of solar light. In many parts of the world at this time, the promise of sunlight seems bleak, even imaginary. The world around us is slowly awakening from its wintery slumber, and some semblance of excitement begins to grow in the hearts of those attuned to the seasonal tides.

Daylight hours are short in February, so this time of year can sometimes feel depressive. We must actively cultivate our inner light through regular exercise, solid sleep, meditation, yoga, ritual, studying, artwork, and planning ahead for the year. When performing magickal work this month, remember that your energy levels may be lower than usual and you must summon your own inner light to strengthen and illuminate your efforts. Do whatever it takes to stay on top of your game, keep energized, cultivate happiness, and embrace February's cleansing rebirth!

Raven Digitalis

February 1
Monday

3rd ♍

☽ v/c 6:10 am

☽ → ♎ 6:25 am

Color of the Day: Silver
Incense of the Day: Rosemary

Imbolc Cleansing

Imbolc is a time of renewal, so run the bathwater and plan for a cleanse. You'll need a tub of hot water, a handful of salt (Epsom, sea, or table salt will do), a scented moisturizer, and candles and incense as desired.

Run the bath. Safely light the candles and incense. Strip off your clothes, and be conscious of what you want to strip away. Perhaps you have a bad habit you want to shed, negative thoughts you want to release, or people you want to leave behind. As the clothes fall to the floor, say:

I am done with this.

Step into the bath. Immerse yourself and soak. Use the salt to scrub from the soles of your feet to the palms of your hands. Salt exfoliates and draws out impurities and negativity.

Rinse yourself with cool water. Drain the tub and watch all the negativity drain away. Anoint yourself with moisturizer. Affirm:

I am cleansed and purified.

Extinguish the candles and incense.

Dallas Jennifer Cobb

February 2
Tuesday

3rd ♎

Color of the Day: Red
Incense of the Day: Ginger

Imbolc – Groundhog Day

Looking at the Future

February 2 is known in the US as Groundhog Day, a modern secular holiday that has its roots in the Pagan holiday of Imbolc. Theoretically, if the groundhog sees his shadow today, winter will last another six weeks. If he doesn't, spring will come early. Either way, he has to leave his burrow to find out.

This is a good day to peek your head out and see what lies ahead in your own near future. Don't worry about the whole year—just focus on what you might expect in the next few months. You can use a tarot or oracle deck, if you are so inclined, or simply light a candle in a firesafe container and focus on your wish to know what the future holds. Then open your mind and heart and say:

Groundhog, groundhog,

Get out of your bed,

And help me to see

Just what lies ahead

Deborah Blake

February 3
Wednesday

3rd ♎

☽ v/c 1:15 am

☽ → ♏ 9:15 am

Color of the Day: Topaz
Incense of the Day: Bay laurel

A Spell to Remember Studied Information

Wednesdays are associated with the god Mercury, thanks to the Romans, who named the days of the week after the gods (as well as the known planets). In French, Wednesday is *mercredi*, and in Spanish it is *miercoles*. In English, however, Wednesday comes from the Old English *Wodensdaeg*, after the Germanic god Woden, or Odin. Both Mercury and Odin are associated with change, the acquisition of knowledge, and wisdom, which makes today a great day for tasks related to research and studying.

Writing something down is proven to be one of the most effective ways of remembering it. To ensure that you retain information you are trying to learn, be sure to read and listen thoroughly, and get in the habit of taking notes. You may enchant your favorite writing utensil by passing it through incense smoke and saying the following:

Lead and ink,

Pen and quill.

All I write,

Recalled at will.

Whatever you write with the utensil will stay in your memory and be easily recited as necessary.

Thorn Mooney

NOTES:

February 4
Thursday

3rd ♏

4th Quarter 12:37 pm

Color of the Day: White
Incense of the Day: Balsam

Snow Fairies

With winter comes snow, and with snow come snow fairies. We have all heard of Jack Frost, but there are many more spirits who deal in ice crystals. They ride the freezing winds of winter to leave frost on the windowpanes. They ice over the lakes and fill the cloudy sky with snowflakes.

To make friends with the snow fairies, collect things that attract them. They love the colors white, silver, and blue. They like crystals and mirrors. Ribbons and bells are also good. You can use snowflake ornaments left over from Yule, snowflake glitter, or confetti. Decorate a corner of a shelf or a shadowbox frame with these things.

After making your display, speak to the snow fairies and admire their beautiful work in the world. Let them know you appreciate the snow that stores water and insulates the ground. If they like you, they may grant favors such as bringing or withholding snow at your request.

Elizabeth Barrette

February 5
Friday

4th ♏

☽ v/c 4:20 am

☽ → ♐ 12:16 pm

Color of the Day: Coral
Incense of the Day: Thyme

The "Craft" in Witchcraft

Are you a painter or sculptor? Do you draw? Can you sew? Are you a writer? I can't sew a straight stitch to save my life, and sewing machines terrify me. But give me a glue gun and some magickal bits of this and that, and I'm ready to go.

There's a reason that the word *craft* is part of the word *Witchcraft*. Witches are crafty. We like doing things with our hands and we like using our minds. For this rite, I'd like to encourage you to do something crafty, whatever or however that shows up for you. And don't worry: there is no need to show your handiwork to anyone. Offer up your creation to the Goddess and know that on this starry night, she is well pleased.

Najah Lightfoot

February 6
Saturday

4th ♐

Color of the Day: Brown
Incense of the Day: Sandalwood

The Blessing of Mercury

The much-dreaded Mercury retrograde need not be the metaphysical villain it's often said to be. Though communications do seem to break down more readily during this period, it's usually not feasible for us to simply avoid communicating with family or coworkers or signing contracts. Mercury will be retrograde until February 20. If we must do these things during this time, we can use magic to help avoid or minimize these issues.

For this spell you will need the following materials:

- A piece of paper
- Scissors
- A pen
- Your shoes
- A glass of wine

Cut the paper into two pieces, each in the shape of a bird's wing. On each piece, draw the symbol for Mercury ($☿$), then place inside your shoes. Now enchant the wine by saying:

God of tricksters, liars, thieves!

Messenger of the divine,

Bestow your blessing upon me, please,

As I offer you this wine.

With your fingers, dab some of the wine on each wing. Offer the rest of the wine by pouring it onto the land. Wear your shoes with confidence.

Storm Faerywolf

Notes:

February 7
Sunday

4th ♐

☽ v/c 1:16 am

☽ → ♑ 3:52 pm

Color of the Day: Orange

Incense of the Day: Juniper

Purify and Balance

Two common kitchen herbs can make purifying your personal space very simple and also bring balance to your environment. Rosemary is associated with the Sun and the element of fire, and thyme is associated with Venus and the element of water. The combination of these two herbs represents a balance of projective and receptive energies—masculine and feminine. In addition, in this spell you're applying heat to water, another way the two elements are blended.

Add equal parts of dried rosemary and dried thyme to a cheesecloth bundle or tea bag. Steep the bag of dried herbs in hot water for five minutes. While the infusion is steeping, chant this phrase and stir the water briefly in a clockwise manner three times:

Water and fire, your balance I require.

Allow the water to cool, then pour it into a spray bottle and use it to mist any place that needs clearing and balance. Visualize negativity being dispelled as you spray the mist. Dispose of the steeped herbs.

Ember Grant

February 8
Monday

4th ♑

Color of the Day: Ivory

Incense of the Day: Narcissus

Modern Anti-Poverty Witch Bottle

This spell is designed to guard against financial hardship. It takes the notion that shredded and torn items corresponding to the goal will magically shred that which we are warding off, in this case poverty. If you don't have credit cards you wish to cut up, bits of hard plastic packaging will do.

Gather these items:

• Red candle in a holder

• Intention scroll: pen, paper, and a green or gold ribbon

• Glass bottle with a lid

• Cut-up credit cards

• Torn bills

• Tulip petals

Light the candle, and on a new piece of paper, write the following intention:

For the good of all, protected I'll be, from financial hardship and poverty; secured and safe, trouble-free, without harm, so mote it be.

Roll this paper up into a scroll and tie it with the ribbon. Add each of the items to the bottle and close it.

Finally, carefully drip wax from the red candle over the bottle lid to fully seal it, activating the magic. Be sure to extinguish the candle.

Michael Furie

NOTES:

 February 9
Tuesday

4th ♑

☽ v/c 12:22 pm

☽ → ♒ 8:20 pm

Color of the Day: White
Incense of the Day: Bayberry

Block Buster Spell

Tuesday, the day of Mars, is always a good time to do work for new beginnings and breakthroughs. Today happens to be a particularly powerful day for this, as Mars is currently transiting Taurus, the sign known for its work ethic. Cast this spell to open the roads that feel blocked to you.

Using a small carving tool, etch the name of the block you wish to bust on the side of a red candle. Dress the candle by rubbing the sides with ground ginger and cinnamon, then affix it to a firesafe dish or candleholder. Facing the west, recite the following spell and then light the candle. Allow the candle to burn completely without snuffing it out.

Tired, over it, I am done with this sh*t,

I call the powers, get me out of this pit.

I banish the blocks and clear the way,

I call in the new, the old cannot stay.

Devin hunter

February 10
Wednesday

4th ≈

Color of the Day: Brown
Incense of the Day: Lilac

End Gossip Spell

If you've been the target of slander and gossip, this spell will help end it. You'll need a blue ink pen, paper, a small freezer bag, and some water.

First, write the rumor on the paper and place it in the freezer bag. Fill the bag with enough water to cover the paper. Toss the bag into your freezer. After the water has frozen, remove the bag from the freezer. Let the bag sit on your counter, or in your sink, until the water has thawed. When thawed, hold the bag and say:

No more slander, no more lies.

Let water turn to ice.

Let ice turn to water.

Only the truth will be told hereafter.

Remove whatever is left of the paper. Throw it away or put it in a compost pile. Pour the water down a drain or on the ground. The gossip should now begin to stop.

James Kambos

 February 11
Thursday

4th ≈

☽ v/c 2:06 pm

New Moon 2:06 pm

Color of the Day: Purple
Incense of the Day: Myrrh

New Moon Love Spell

Since today is the new moon, it is a perfect time to attract new love. Fill your tub with water for a cleansing, magical bath. On the edge of the tub place rose quartz crystals to enhance unconditional love for yourself and others, along with clear quartz crystals to amplify that intention. In the bathwater, add white rose petals for purity, yellow rose petals for joy and friendship, lavender rose petals for magical enchantment, orange rose petals for passion, and red rose petals for love. Take a deep breath, relax, inhale the scent of the flowers, and soak up the divine earth love. Clear your mind and your heart, then say these words:

On this new moon night,
my love burns bright.

Attract the love to me
that is my destiny.

Remove the flower petals and place them on your altar to dry. Once they have dried, take them outside and toss them into the wind to send your wishes for love into the air.

Sapphire Moonbeam

 ## February 12
Friday

1st ≈

☽ → ♓ 2:23 am

Color of the Day: Rose
Incense of the Day: Alder

Lunar New Year (Ox)

Year of the Ox

Today is Lunar New Year! In Chinese astrology, it is the year of the Ox. The Chinese consider the Ox to be hardworking, reliable, and intelligent. Perhaps you'd like to take hold of the auspicious energies of this day and channel them into beginning a project you have been thinking about embarking upon. Find an image online of an Ox that you can print and place on your altar, and light a candle before it. Meditate on the qualities of the Ox, and recite an intention similar to the following:

Lunar power glowing bright,

This is the year of the Ox's might!

Earthy and honest, reliable and keen,

May great progress on
my venture be seen!

Let the candle burn down safely in an appropriate holder. While it burns, take steps to begin your project. Keep the picture of the Ox to remind you of your goals and to help you remain steady in your efforts.

Blake Octavian Blair

February 13
Saturday

1st ♓

Color of the Day: Gray
Incense of the Day: Pine

Waxing Moon Money Spell

Draw a picture of a waxing moon (☽) on the palm of your hand with henna or marker. If you don't want anyone to see it, you can instead draw it on a hidden part of your body.

As you draw the outline of the crescent moon and then color it in, visualize prosperity entering your life. See yourself paying the bills and buying the things you want and need, and feel how relieved and happy you'll be when this happens. If you use henna, it will have to sit on your skin until it dries. Spend this time visualizing your goal as if you already have it. You can even imagine a stack of money sitting in the palm of your hand.

When the moon picture has dried, go about your business and forget about it. Wash your hands as usual, and allow it to naturally fade away. By the next full moon, some money should come your way.

Kate Freuler

February 14
Sunday

1st ♓

☽ v/c 2:29 am

☽ → ♈ 10:54 am

Color of the Day: Gold
Incense of the Day: Eucalyptus

Valentine's Day

Platonic Love

People usually think of Valentine's Day as a holiday of lust and romance, but love is so much more than those things. There are many more kinds of love, platonic as well as carnal. Today is a good time to celebrate them as well.

You will need a piece of parchment paper, a pen, ink, and a ribbon. Use Dove's Blood magical ink if you have it. Otherwise, use ordinary ink in a color you associate with love. On one side of the paper, write down all the kinds of love you can think of: love of parent for child, love of child for parent, love between siblings, love between friends, and so on. On the other side of the paper, write the names of the people you love and who love you. If you don't want to use names, descriptions or roles work fine. Then roll up the paper and tie it with the ribbon. Carry it with you or keep it on your altar as a concrete symbol of love.

Elizabeth Barrette

♥ **February 15**
Monday

1st ♈

Color of the Day: Lavender
Incense of the Day: Clary sage

Presidents' Day

A Breakup Spell

Valentine's Day has come and gone, and many of us may be glad to see it go. Sometimes romantic love is the last thing you need, especially if the relationship is toxic, limiting, or just long past its expiration date. The best way to break up with someone is almost always face-to-face, with directness and honesty, but a little magical help can ease the process.

On a slip of paper, write down your grievances. Focus on your own feelings and experiences. After all, you can only control yourself, not your partner! You can make a list or create a picture or sigil instead. When you're finished, safely burn the paper in a heatproof dish or cauldron, visualizing the relationship ending smoothly. Say:

Go quickly, go completely,
go in peace. I release you.

Scatter the ashes in the wind or bury them far away from where you live (maybe in a public park or a forest, where the energy can dissipate safely and you aren't trespassing). You want this relationship out of your life, so make sure the spell remains are nowhere near your home!

Thorn Mooney

Notes:

 February 16
Tuesday

1st ♈

☽ v/c 7:17 pm

☽ → ♉ 10:12 pm

Color of the Day: Scarlet
Incense of the Day: Cedar

Mardi Gras (Fat Tuesday)

Let the Good Times Roll

Today is all about breaking the mold and is the ideal day to drink rum and eat bananas, pudding with coconut rice, and King Cake for breakfast, lunch, and dinner! Live for the little joys in life with this French prayer and with purple and green candles on a cake fit for a king. Give yourself permission to feel happy and alive, even if only for today. As you light the candles on the cake, say:

> *Elever votre esprit et laissez les bons temps rouler!*

> (Lift up your spirits and let the good times roll.)

Buy your cake from an artisan baker and make a point to go out into a community of artists and performers to show them your support. Enjoy the spirit of live music in an effort to let loose, and allow yourself to dance! There is no better time to enjoy life than at this very moment, fleeting and precious as it is.

Estha McNevin

February 17
Wednesday

1st ♉

Color of the Day: White
Incense of the Day: Lavender

Ash Wednesday

Ashes to Ashes, Dust to Dust

On this day you may come across people with ashes on their forehead. The practice is rooted in antiquity and symbolizes mortality, faith, and the beginning of Lent. While this practice is commonly associated with people who are Christian, we too as Pagan or earth-based spiritual people can connect with our mortality and humility by placing a bit of dirt on our forehead. You can choose to make your forehead symbol any form that calls to you.

For this spell, gather a bit of earth. Hold the earth in the palm of your hand. Breathe in its earthy goodness. Say:

From the earth I came, unto the
earth I shall return. I am loved,
guided, blessed, and protected.

Now place a bit of the earth on your forehead. Allow it to remain there until you are ready to remove it.

Najah Lightfoot

February 18
Thursday

1st ♉

☉ → ♓ 5:44 am

Color of the Day: Green
Incense of the Day: Carnation

Water from the Sky

For most of us, February is a month when water comes from the sky in one form or another. In California, that may be rain. In New York, it's usually snow. Either way, this is a good time to embrace water's gifts, even if they make life a little more challenging. After all, water is the basis of life.

So instead of bemoaning the precipitation, collect a little bit in a bowl and use it for this simple spell. Hold the bowl between your hands and lift it to the sky. If you want, you can dab a little water on your brow, your lips, your heart, and your core. Then say:

Water, wet and full of power,

Lend me energy in this hour.

Fuel my body, mind, and soul

With the water in this bowl.

Feel the energy moving from the water, down your arms, and into your body. You can save the rest and use it for your magical work, or pour it back outside.

Deborah Blake

February 19
Friday

1st ♉

☽ v/c 2:28 am

☽ → ♊ 11:04 am

2nd Quarter 1:47 pm

Color of the Day: Pink
Incense of the Day: Mint

A Mercurial Soul Retrieval

Mercury is still retrograde until tomorrow. Let's make it work for us instead of against us. This is a good time to reflect on past events that still need resolution. These are parts of our soul that are "trapped" in our past, meaning we do not have access to the life force that is contained within them. But if we can call them back to us and confront them, we can reclaim our stolen power.

For this spell you will need a white candle. Ground and center. Think of a past event that has caused you trouble. Light the candle and say:

Shadow rooted in the past,

With this light be guided home.

Contemplate the past issue. Feel whatever emotions that arise. While in this space, imagine the light of the candle permeating the memory and the associated emotions, guiding the energy back to you as you breathe it in. Allow the candle to burn down safely.

Storm Faerywolf

February 20
Saturday

2nd ♊

Color of the Day: Indigo
Incense of the Day: Rue

Mercury Retrograde Ends

Today marks the end of the first Mercury retrograde of 2021. Breathe a sigh of relief as this planet goes direct today and communication gets back on track. Now is the time to review and send those missives you've been holding onto for fear of being misunderstood. Call friends and get back into the swing of things socially. Complete the projects that have been on hold. Go ahead and make plans for vacations or business trips.

Mercury retrograde is a time to pause and reflect on communication in all forms. Offer up gratitude for having gotten through it once more, with all good thoughts and positive energy.

Emyme

February 21
Sunday

2nd ♊

☽ v/c 1:39 pm

☽ → ♋ 10:53 pm

Color of the Day: Amber
Incense of the Day: Marigold

Feralia

On this day, ancient Rome had a festival called Feralia that was somewhat like the Day of the Dead. This marked the end of the nine-day festival Parentalia. It was a traditional time to honor one's ancestors and pay homage to them. *Ferre* means "to carry" or "to ferry," as in ferrying the dead across the river to the underworld. According to Ovid, people would visit tombs with offerings to appease the ghosts. Gifts included flowers, wine-soaked pieces of bread, salt, or grain.

Today, if possible, visit the grave of someone you have lost and bring a small token. If this isn't possible, create a place of honor for them on your altar instead. Decorate it with images of your ancestors and items that you associate with them. Take time today to remember those you've lost.

Ember Grant

February 22
Monday

2nd ♋

Color of the Day: White
Incense of the Day: Hyssop

Elemental Protection

Sybil Leek was an astrologer, a psychic, and a witch, and today was her birthday. With her jackdaw bird and flowing cape, she was an early, visible witch and mystic who, like Gerald Gardener, was one of the first to publish books on witchcraft.

Today, let's cast a circle of protection around ourselves, our familiars, our circles, and our Pagan path so that all witches and practitioners of the craft are free to practice.

As you face each direction, use your right index finger to draw a pentagram for protection in the air as you say the following words.

In the east:

May air inspire deep breaths, diversity, and acceptance of all.

In the south:

May fire burn away intolerance, warming our hands, heads, and hearts.

In the west:

May water balm all old wounds, bringing spiritual healing.

In the north:

May the earth uphold and support us all.

To the center:

May all Pagans live in peace. Blessed be.

Dallas Jennifer Cobb

NOTES:

 February 23
Tuesday

2nd ♋

☽ v/c 11:54 pm

Color of the Day: Maroon
Incense of the Day: Basil

Magically Enhanced Water

There is so much focus now on different types of water: bottled water, vitamin-enriched water, spring water, mineral water, etc. All of these are great, but magical people can take things even further. Water is so receptive that it can be programmed with an intention and then, when drunk, this magic is internalized to create its effect.

To program the water, pour the desired amount into a cup or pitcher and hold your hands over it while willing your intention into the liquid. You can then drink as much of it as you wish. Additionally, club soda can be added for a power boost, or fresh produce can be added for a variety of intentions, such as fresh cucumbers for healing and moon magic, cherries for love energy, blueberries or huckleberries for cleansing and protection, or lemon and lime for purification. You can experiment to find your favorite combinations.

Michael Furie

February 24
Wednesday

2nd ♋

☽ → ♌ 7:23 am

Color of the Day: Brown
Incense of the Day: Honeysuckle

Love Renewal

Dragobete is a traditional Romanian holiday celebrated on February 24. Dragobete is the patron saint of love and cheerfulness as well as the patron saint of birds. This holiday is a day for lovers and a celebration of the rebirth of nature. The patron saint Dragobete reminds us to never stop celebrating love.

Place spring flowers, flower petals, and bird feathers that you find in nature in a circle on your altar or sacred space. In the middle of the circle place one white candle. As the candle burns, visualize love renewed, whether the love is old or new. Chant these words:

May my love be renewed, may the feathers help me fly, may my joy reach the greatest heights in the sky.

While my white candle burns and reflects the purity in my heart, I desire that my love will have a fresh new start.

Be sure to blow out the candle after the chant.

Sapphire Moonbeam

February 25
Thursday

2nd ♌

Color of the Day: Turquoise
Incense of the Day: Mulberry

Venus in Pisces Relationship Spell

Venus makes its move into Pisces today, and for the next month or so, people may be more sensitive or more aware of what they need from each other, and we can expect to have some deeper relationship-oriented conversations. Cast this spell to harmonize with this energy and to ensure positive outcomes from potentially upsetting interactions.

On a 4 by 4-inch piece of parchment paper, draw the symbol of Venus (♀) in red ink. Rotate the paper clockwise 180 degrees, then draw the symbol of Pisces (♓)over the symbol of Venus. Rotate the paper clockwise 90 degrees and fold it toward you, then repeat two more times (three folds). Kiss the folded paper and say:

From up and down and all around,

I harmonize with Venus and Pisces.

Heart to heart, matters won't part,

We shall live through any crises!

Keep the parchment in your wallet or purse.

Devin Hunter

February 26
Friday

2nd ♌

☽ v/c 6:32 am

☽ → ♍ 12:07 pm

Color of the Day: Purple
Incense of the Day: Violet

Purim begins at sundown

Awaken the Sun and Earth Spell

At this time of year we begin to grow anxious and are ready for spring. This spell will help keep you in step with the natural world. It will also make you feel that you're hurrying spring along.

You'll need an orange candle, a houseplant, and a watering can. Place the candle, the plant, and the watering can filled with water on your altar. Begin by saying:

Sun, awaken and rise into the sky.

Show me your light and power.

Earth, awaken from your frosty grave.

*Show me your green grass
and begin to flower.*

Next, safely light the candle and water the plant. Visualize the sun growing in strength and the earth turning green again. When you're ready, snuff out the candle. This ends the spell. Perform this ritual as often as you like until the days are mild again.

James Kambos

 February 27
Saturday

2nd ♍

Full Moon 3:17 am

Color of the Day: Blue
Incense of the Day: Ivy

Snow Moon Cleanse

The February full moon is often referred to as the Snow Moon. Take advantage of today's special energies to cleanse any water-safe crystals and tools you want to recharge. If you live in a snowy climate, fill a bowl with snow from the ground. Place the water-safe objects in it and leave the bowl out under the moonlight overnight. If you live in a climate that does not receive snow, you can place snowflake obsidian stones in the water to carry and honor the energy of snow. After you place the objects in the bowl, you can say a blessing such as this:

Full Snow Moon,

I ask of thee,

*Please cleanse and imbue
with your unique energy.*

So mote it be!

In the morning, retrieve your objects and dry them.

Blake Octavian Blair

February 28
Sunday

3rd ♏

☽ v/c 10:58 am

☽ → ♎ 2:17 pm

Color of the Day: Yellow
Incense of the Day: Heliotrope

Muting Spell

Sometimes we have to spend time with difficult people whether we like it or not. Opinions clash. Personalities don't mix. It's just part of life. When you find yourself having to be around an abrasive or annoying personality, use this onion spell to mute their energy so you can get on with your day.

You will need an onion, a knife, and a jar with a tight lid. Cut the ends off the onion and peel it. It will stink and make your eyes water; this symbolizes the offensive behavior of the person and your reaction to them. Tolerate it for as long as you can while visualizing their actions. Then put the onion in the jar and seal the lid. Notice that the impact of the onion is now muted, no longer affecting your sinuses or eyes. Imagine that the person's energy, voice, and presence are muted too, as if they're behind glass.

Put the jar away out of sight. When the situation has resolved, compost the onion and wash the jar well.

Kate Freuler

March

March is upon us! March is a month of unpredictable weather. Will the weather spirits decide to bring us a last hurrah of winter in the form of a blustery snowstorm or instead bring us signs of spring's beginning in the form of budding trees and perhaps rain showers sprinkled with mild, sunny days? There really is no telling! However, for those of us who follow the Wheel of the Year, the spring equinox is a time of new beginnings, regardless of the weather.

Rituals of spring and new beginnings will take place around the globe this month. Druids still gather at Stonehenge to welcome the rising sun on the morning of the equinox. March also is the time to celebrate the festival of Holi, popular in India and Nepal. People engage in paint fights, covering each other in festive splatters of vibrant color, welcoming the arrival of spring and all its vibrancy.

In March, however you choose to celebrate, work the magick of new beginnings!

Blake Octavian Blair

 March 1
Monday

3rd ♎

Color of the Day: Gray
Incense of the Day: Lily

To Soothe Emotional Upheaval

Today the moon is in powerful Libra, which may bring a bit of internal upheaval as we compare ourselves to the world around us. Our sense of right and wrong and how that fits into our reality may be at odds at this time. Cast this spell to decrease the intensity and to help smooth out any mental/emotional frustrations you may be experiencing.

Fill a bucket or your bathtub with warm water, just enough to cover your foot. Place one foot in the warm water, with the other remaining on dry land, and say:

Salty water and dry land, these two worlds I have in hand.

Soothing waves and changing tide, from within I cannot hide.

Balance in the place of strife, bringing strength into this life.

It is my will, so must it be, with this spell I shall be free!

Devin Hunter

 March 2
Tuesday

3rd ♎

☽ v/c 9:09 am
☽ → ♏ 3:38 pm

Color of the Day: Scarlet
Incense of the Day: Cinnamon

Snow Problem at All

By this time of year, most people are tired of the winter cold and are ready for spring to arrive. Since spring is still a few weeks away, we can harness the energy of this last bit of winter to remove a problem or obstacle from our lives.

Create a symbol of the problem you wish to remove, or write down the problem on a piece of paper and fold it into a small square, making each fold away from you. If you live where there is snow, gather some into a freezer-safe container (with a lid) and bring it indoors. If not, use some crushed ice. Bury the symbol or paper deep in the center of the snow or ice and place the lid on tight. Put the container in the freezer with these words:

Power of winter, this issue resolve, freeze, remove, scatter, dissolve.

Freed from the problem and balance achieved, my gratitude I give for this blessing received.

Michael Furie

March 3
Wednesday

3rd ♏

Color of the Day: Yellow
Incense of the Day: Marjoram

Fire Spell to Banish Debt

Many of us receive and pay bills electronically now, so use a sheet of paper for this spell if necessary to represent a bill you're having trouble paying off. Write the name of the bill on the paper. Of course, if you have a paper bill or statement, use that. Light a candle in a large heatproof dish or cauldron and carefully pass the blades of a pair of scissors through the fire several times. Visualize the blades becoming empowered with the element of fire. Then cut the paper (or bill) into small pieces with the scissors. Every time you cut, see your debt being snipped into smaller and more manageable pieces. When the paper is completely cut into pieces, scoop them up and burn them in the fire. (You may want to do this spell outside or use a fire pit.) As you toss the pieces into the fire, speak these words:

> I can manage this debt;
> it's no longer a threat.

Be sure to extinguish the fire.

Ember Grant

 March 4
Thursday

3rd ♏
☽ v/c 11:10 am
☽ → ♐ 5:43 pm

Color of the Day: Crimson
Incense of the Day: Jasmine

The Luck of a Green-Clad Leprechaun

According to myth, a leprechaun's tweed is green for those folks who like to socialize and red for those who write manifestos on the overpopulation of the human species. The red-clad leprechauns are best left alone at home, to toil away by the light of an earwax lamp. A green-clad leprechaun, however, can be anyone, anywhere, at any time; you may not even know he's been for tea but for the simple fact that he left you lucky!

Hang a small child-size green tweed jacket by your back door to entice a lucky leprechaun to visit and bless you and your house. Keep his coat by the back door so he knows he's welcome as one of the family. Place a sweet bun or candy in the left pocket and, if possible, a four-leaf clover in the right. Leave kind messages and three wishes for him, along with some treats to win his favor.

Estha McNevin

March 5
Friday

3rd ♐
4th Quarter 8:30 pm
Color of the Day: Purple
Incense of the Day: Yarrow

A Sea Spirit Spell

Traditionally in ancient times this date marked the beginning of the sailing season in the eastern Mediterranean Sea. Sailors prayed and blessings were said for a safe and bountiful year at sea. Utilize the energies of this day by performing this spell to bring you some prosperity.

You'll need a plain white sheet of paper, a blue crayon, a pen, and a few drops of salt water. At the top of the paper, draw a wave design using the crayon. If you wish, you may also add other sea-related designs, such as a ship, a dolphin, a fish, etc. Beneath the design write this charm in ink:

Spirits of the sand, spirits of the sea,

Favor me with prosperity.

Now read the charm aloud. Sprinkle the paper with a few drops of salt water. Fold the paper like a letter and hide it. When good fortune begins to come to you, give thanks, then discard the paper.

James Kambos

 ## March 6
Saturday

4th ♐
☽ v/c 4:44 am
☽ → ♑ 9:20 pm

Color of the Day: Black
Incense of the Day: Magnolia

Mad as a March hare

You may have heard this old expression, which originated in England and is best known to most people through the character of the March Hare in *Alice in Wonderland*. The saying comes from the unpredictable behavior of the hare, or wild rabbit, during its mating season in March. You might think this is a bad thing, but if you've been in a relationship for a while, you might be feeling the need for a little fanciful madness of your own.

To bring a little passion to your relationship, try putting a carved figure or a picture of a rabbit on your altar (maybe along with a carrot as an offering) and asking the gods for some new ideas to bring fire to an old love:

Make me mad as a hare

Now that spring's in the air.

Breathe new life into love

With a spark from above.

Deborah Blake

March 7
Sunday

4th ♑

Color of the Day: Gold
Incense of the Day: Almond

Bitter Seeds Banishing Spell

Apple seeds not only are bitter to taste but contain a miniscule amount of poison. (Don't worry, it's not enough to harm you.) This toxic quality makes them useful in banishing spells.

On tonight's waning moon, consider a personal issue or situation that's been bothering you, making you feel bitter or sour. Gather three apples seeds and find a quiet spot where you won't be disturbed.

Hold the seeds in your hand. Allow yourself to feel the bitterness and negative feelings as they come over you. Mentally direct those feelings into the seeds. You can do this by visualizing a trail of black smoke drifting from your heart into the pips. Do this for as long as necessary, until the feeling of unhappiness starts to diminish or you lose focus.

Now take the seeds outdoors under the waning moon. Throw them away from you onto the earth, separating yourself from the black smoky energy. They will either deteriorate and be composted into new life, or they will sprout and grow, transforming into something useful.

Kate Freuler

March 8
Monday

4th ♑
☽ v/c 7:52 pm

Color of the Day: White
Incense of the Day: Rosemary

Celebrating International Women's Day

Today is International Women's Day, a time to stop and recognize the important accomplishments of women in the arenas of politics, human rights, economics, etc. Today, don't simply celebrate on the macrocosmic level; bring your acknowledgments down into the microcosm of your life. Take the time to directly acknowledge an individual woman you know personally and thank her for her efforts. Those who fight in the name of progress are often happy to do the job but will tell you it is thankless work. Gratitude is a kind of magic all its own, and expressing it is an act of magic. If the woman is living, email, call, or visit her. Let her know you appreciate her efforts. Perhaps bake her a treat or get her a cup of coffee in appreciation. If the woman has passed, make an offering to her spirit.

Blake Octavian Blair

March 9
Tuesday

4th ♑

☽ → ♒ 2:41 am

Color of the Day: Red
Incense of the Day: Cedar

Goddess Caffeina

Teas and coffees wake us up and enliven our spirit. However, not all of us are coffee or tea drinkers. Some people grab an energy shot to begin their day.

But before you pour that liquid caffeine into your mouth, in whatever form you like best, take a moment to give thanks to the goddess Caffeina, mother of caffeinated drinks.

Before one sip of that delicious libation touches your lips, say:

Goddess Caffeina, I honor you. Unto you, Mother Earth, I give the first sip of this delicious drink, which stirs my being and shakes my soul. Thank you for the blessing of caffeine!

After you have finished saying your blessing, pour a bit of your drink onto the earth.

Now go forth and enjoy your caffeinated drink!

Najah Lightfoot

March 10
Wednesday

4th ♒

☽ v/c 10:32 pm

Color of the Day: Brown
Incense of the Day: Lilac

Strengthen the Bonds of Friendship

For this spell you will need the following materials:

- One fresh cut flower for each person in the friendship
- Several pieces of paper
- A pen
- A large, heavy book (An old dictionary or phone book works best.)
- A needle and thread

Choose a flower for each person in the friendship. Bonus points for choosing their favorite flower.

Perform the following steps for each individual involved, including yourself. Take two pieces of paper. On each, write the person's name thirteen times. Hold the flower and focus your attention on it. Imagine that the person is emerging from the flower. Say:

By stem and petal, leaf and bud,

Unfolding flower, I name you
_____ *(name of person).*

Place the flower between the two sheets of paper and insert them into the book. Firmly close the book.

Repeat these steps until each person has a flower in the book. Now collect the papers and sew them all together in any fashion you choose while you chant:

*Friends through thick and
friends through thin.*

Keep the papers and flowers hidden away.

Storm Faerywolf

NOTES:

 March 11
Thursday

4th ≈
☽ → ♓ 9:44 am

Color of the Day: Green
Incense of the Day: Myrrh

Listen to Your Instincts

Some days you wake up energized for a new venture or the completion of a project, and ready to accomplish anything, but your calendar is full of obligations. There comes a time and place to listen to your body and soul and point that energy inward.

Try this today. First perform whatever morning ritual you have. Then contact those to whom you have obligations—work, family, friends—and cancel those plans. Next, plant yourself in front of your chosen task and ready, set, go! My personal preparation on such days includes candles for aromatherapy and a request to the appropriate goddess or muse, such as this one:

*(Name of goddess or muse), I thank
you for your inspiration. Allow
the creativity to flow through me.
Guide my hands in the performance
of this work in your honor.*

All is well. Blessed be.

Emyme

March 12
Friday

4th ♓

Color of the Day: Pink
Incense of the Day: Orchid

Divining Rods Spell

There is much talk these days about food sensitivities. Using divining rods can help put the power of diagnosis in your own hands.

Create a set of divining rods using two 20-inch lengths of medium-gauge aluminum (from a hardware store) or straightened coat-hanger wire. Bend each wire into an *L* shape, with a 5-inch "arm." Hold the two arms loosely in your closed hands so that the 15-inch length of each rod floats horizontally in front of you.

Experiment with foods that you know disagree with you until you understand what "bad" looks like with your rods. My rods push out wide to the sides to indicate "bad" foods. Once you have established what "good" and "bad" look like, use the rods to connect to your own higher knowing and cellular vibration, and test foods to confirm what is problematic for your system. Seeing is believing and hearing your higher self.

Dallas Jennifer Cobb

 March 13
Saturday

4th ♓
New Moon 5:21 am
☽ v/c 11:38 am
☽ → ♈ 6:44 pm

Color of the Day: Blue
Incense of the Day: Patchouli

Truth Honey

There is nothing kinder than a truth from a friend delivered with tact and pure love. It can be hard to speak our mind. This little potion helps to sweeten the tongue, making it easier to express our compassion and sincerity. Enjoy a spoonful of this elixir before any heart-to-heart, and it will make for honesty and golden communication, rooted in perfect love and perfect trust.

Gather the following ingredients:

- 2 cups honey
- 1 cup apple juice
- 4 quince, sliced
- 8 juniper berries, dried
- ¼ teaspoon jasmine flowers
- 8 slices fresh or canned lotus root

Combine all of the ingredients, warming them over low heat. Cook this on low for 1.5 hours or until the fruit begins to mash when pressed. Strain into a glass jar and feed the pulp to wild creatures. Draw or decorate the jar with lotus flowers, yin-yang symbols, and peace signs to further imbibe the elixir.

Estha McNevin

NOTES:

March 14
Sunday

1st ♈

Color of the Day: Yellow
Incense of the Day: Frankincense

Daylight Saving Time
begins at 2:00 a.m.

Butterfly Magick

March 14 is Learn About Butterflies Day. Butterflies are a universal symbol of transformation. When you encounter butterflies on a regular basis, it is a message from spirit that big changes are on the way. In order to harness the energy of the butterfly, you can perform this simple spell. Gather seasonal flowers and place them on your altar or sacred space along with labradorite (a transformation stone) and quartz crystals (to amplify your intentions). Say these words and repeat as many times as needed:

> May the wings of the butterfly
> set me free and allow wonderful
> changes to come to me.

> I will flow with the transformation
> without a care, like the butterfly
> as it flies gracefully in the air.

Release your expectation to the outcome of the changes you desire and trust that the universe will guide you to your highest good.

Sapphire Moonbeam

March 15
Monday

1st ♈

☽ v/c 11:40 pm

Color of the Day: Silver
Incense of the Day: Neroli

Spring Cleaning

Spring cleaning is an old tradition. Each year, the old leaves decay and the soil brings forth new flowers. As the world turns bright and colorful again, it encourages us to brush away the remains of the old year and make room for the new. Think about what needs the most attention in your life. Here are some ideas.

In the yard, rake mulch off the flower beds to allow sprouts to come up. Put the old mulch on the compost pile.

Pick up sticks to make a bonfire. You can also pile them into a wildlife shelter.

In the house, sweep any smooth floors and carry out the dust. Vacuum or shampoo carpeted floors.

Then cleanse the area with floor wash. You can buy one (like Chinese wash) from a magical supplier, or make your own with water, sea salt, lemon juice, and the herbal powder or essential oil of your choice.

Sort through your closet and give away at least one bag of unneeded clothes. This encourages abundance.

Elizabeth Barrette

March 16
Tuesday

1st ♈

☽ → ♉ 6:56 am

Color of the Day: Maroon
Incense of the Day: Ginger

A Charm to Work Your Will

Tuesdays are ruled by Mars (in French, Tuesday is called *mardi*), which makes today an auspicious time to work magic pertaining to passion, the will, and any matter that requires fiery, forceful energy. Some of us are naturally forceful, but practically everyone could use a leg up from time to time in order to win in a stressful situation. To encourage outspokenness and the wherewithal to see your will worked in a contested situation, make a sachet that contains ingredients associated with fire, passion, and victory in conflict.

Take a square of red fabric (or a small red pouch, if you have one). Lay it out flat, and in the center place a clove of garlic and a pinch each of ground cinnamon, nettle (dried or fresh), and basil (dried or fresh). Sprinkle the mixture with a pinch of ground cayenne pepper and say:

By the powers of Mars, my will is true.

I find success in all I do.

Tie the sachet with red string or cord and carry it with you throughout your day.

Thorn Mooney

March 17
Wednesday

1st ♉

Color of the Day: Topaz
Incense of the Day: Honeysuckle

Saint Patrick's Day

A March Wind Spell

It's Saint Patrick's Day. The earth is turning green and there's a feeling of celebration in the air. This is a good day to combine the joyous mood and the forces of the March wind to bring a positive change into your life. The winds of March are all about change, as winter turns to spring. Use these winds to remove negativity from your life.

For this ritual you'll need a small rock. It can be any rock that appeals to you. Go to a place where you'll be alone, such as a hilltop, a meadow, or your back yard. Hold your rock and think of the negative issue you wish to be rid of. Face east and say:

East wind, blow away _____
(name the problem).

Then repeat for each other wind direction in this order: south, west, and north. End by facing east again. Now declare yourself free of your problem. Leave your rock as an offering and walk away.

James Kambos

March 18
Thursday

1st ♉

☽ v/c 4:40 pm

☽ → ♊ 7:47 pm

Color of the Day: Turquoise
Incense of the Day: Clove

Prosperity Spell

For this spell you'll need three almonds, preferably raw ones. Wrap the almonds in a dollar bill and tape the ends closed so you have a tube. Carry it with you for seven full days and put it in your pillow case each night. On the morning of the eighth day, open the tube. On this day you must bury the three almonds and spend the dollar. As you bury the almonds (preferably in your yard or in a potted plant), visualize planting seeds of prosperity that will expand and return to you. Say these words as you plant:

By my hands, my prosperity expands.

When you spend the dollar, say these words:

As I spend, my prosperity extends.

Ember Grant

March 19
Friday

1st ♊

Color of the Day: Coral
Incense of the Day: Alder

Planting Seeds of Abundance

Depending on where in the country you live, it may be time to start the first seeds in pots that will eventually be moved outside. Even if you aren't a gardener, it's never too early to plant seeds of prosperity and abundance. March is a good time to plan for the rest of the year, both financially and spiritually, although you can do this spell in any season. You will need a small pot, some potting soil, a few seeds (simple herbs you might use in the kitchen are good, or easy flowers like marigolds), and a shiny penny to symbolize the abundance you desire. Put the coin in the bottom of the pot, add the soil, then place the seeds one by one as you say:

I plant the seeds of wealth and plenty,

Abundance shining like a penny.

Prosperity will grow and grow,

With these seeds that I do sow.

Deborah Blake

March 20
Saturday

1st ♊

☉ → ♈ 5:37 am

Color of the Day: Brown
Incense of the Day: Sandalwood

Spring Equinox – Ostara

Spring Equinox

The center of the visible sun is directly above the earth's equator today, bringing balance and renewal to our energetic world. Day and night are equal in length, and the power to reveal the potential of the coming season is in our hands.

Grab your favorite oracle system (tarot, oracle cards, runes, etc.) and a yellow candle of any size and something to burn it in. Then cast this spell to hone in on the spiritual themes that await you. Light the candle, take three deep breaths, and say:

No more guesses and no more tries,

Show me where the lesson lies.

Reveal the teachings meant for me,

Lift the veil so I can see.

Draw three cards or runes. The first represents your current position. The second represents the spiritual focus that is to come. The third represents what changes must be made in order to successfully move through that lesson. Allow the candle to safely burn out on its own.

Devin Hunter

March 21
Sunday

1st ♊

☽ v/c 8:04 am

☽ → ♋ 8:18 am

2nd Quarter 10:40 am

Color of the Day: Orange
Incense of the Day: Juniper

To Summon Up Calm and Patience

Life has a way of being full-on! Take a minute today to lower your blood pressure by recharging with this Chinese remedy. Tea is comfort from a cup and is especially kind to the kidneys, bladder, and feminine reproductive system. Known for treating hypertension and easing body and mental distress, this blend can stop hot flashes, anxiety, and panic attacks, making it a must-have for any botanical first aid box. Add half a teaspoon to a cup of hot water and let Empress Wu and Mother Nature give you the personal strength to fight off the inner basilisk and work like a boss!

- 2 ounces blue thistle, chopped (dried flowers and leaves)

- ½ ounce violet (dry flowers)

- 1 ounce hibiscus (dry flowers)

- ½ ounce almonds, peeled and slivered

- 2 teaspoons angelica root powder

- 3 teaspoons fresh orange zest

- 2 teaspoons tulsi (holy basil)

- 2 ounces Yun Wu green tea

Estha McNevin

NOTES:

March 22
Monday

2nd ♋

Color of the Day: Lavender
Incense of the Day: Narcissus

The Remember Yourself Spell

A concept that I usually choose to follow in my practice is the idea that spells should be cast "for the good of all." That way, money magic and even binding or banishing (for example) are given the built-in condition that the goal will be achieved without harmful side effects. That being said, it's important to avoid becoming so focused on everyone else's good that you overlook yourself; "all" includes you. This spell serves to ensure that you remain looped in to your own work while simultaneously programming your future magic to be infused with the proper level of care.

Anoint a white candle with a bit of your saliva and place it in a holder. You can burn rosemary incense if you wish. As you light the candle, say:

> *Achieving goals with grace and*
> *charm, commanding, strong, and*
> *without harm; for good of all,*
> *including me, as I will, so mote it be.*

Extinguish with a candle snuffer.

Michael Furie

 ## March 23
Tuesday

2nd ♋

☽ v/c 11:26 am

☽ → ♌ 5:56 pm

Color of the Day: Gray
Incense of the Day: Geranium

Near Miss Day

On this date in 1989, an asteroid came very close to hitting the earth. Since then, people have celebrated March 23 as Near Miss Day.

What other near misses have you or your loved ones experienced? Tainted food? Car accident? Kitchen mishap? Those experiences stay with us long after the actual event. Take some time today to ponder those events and your good fortune, and perhaps write about them.

Soteria is the Greek goddess of safety, deliverance, and protection from hurt, and Soter is her male counterpart. Express gratitude for your near misses and call upon Soteria and Soter and/or the Lady and Lord to continue to offer their protection:

> *In great thanks for the protection*
> *from any "almost" injurious*
> *occasion, we ask to be kept well*
> *and whole going forward.*

Emyme

March 24
Wednesday

2nd ♌

Color of the Day: White
Incense of the Day: Lavender

Obtain the Blessing of a Sylph

Sylphs are elemental points of consciousness that exist within what we experience as the air. When we tune into them, they can help us become cleansed, alert, and revitalized.

For this spell you will need some light-smelling incense and some small wind chimes (or small bells).

Sometime in the morning, face east and light the incense. Ground and center. Imagine the light of the morning sun shining into your heart center. Imagine that the breeze, wind, and clouds are flowing through you. Say:

Morning sun and breath of life,

Vital essence, sing thy song.

Now blow upon the wind chimes (or strike the bells) and imagine that the sound is ringing inside your body as you breathe. Be aware of how the air around you is filled with tiny points of consciousness. You might imagine them as little silver spirals, but just notice however they manifest for you. Imagine breathing them in and out again, leaving you feeling refreshed and cleansed. When finished, be sure to extinguish the incense.

Storm Faerywolf

March 25
Thursday

2nd ♌

☽ v/c 9:27 am

☽ → ♍ 11:25 pm

Color of the Day: Purple
Incense of the Day: Carnation

Turn Left

Today we are going to practice divination by using our intuition. If you always go up the stairs, go down the stairs. If you always sit in a certain chair, sit in a different one. If you always go home by the same route, take a different one today.

What you are doing is waking up your intuition and encouraging spirit to speak to you through the simple act of changing up your routine. We all get into ruts. It may be quicker, faster, or easier to always do things the same way, but what if something magickal and spectacular is waiting for you around the corner or comes your way because you took a different route?

Pay attention to any signs, feelings, nudges, or small miracles that come your way. At the end of the day, notice how changing your routine for just one day brought blessings into your life.

Najah Lightfoot

March 26
Friday

2nd ♏

Color of the Day: Rose
Incense of the Day: Cypress

Remembering the Ancestors of the Land

Today is Prince Kuhio Day. Prince Jonah Kuhio Kalanianaole was a Hawaiian monarch who helped pass the Hawaiian Homes Act, which set aside 200,000 acres of land to be homesteaded by native Hawaiians. We often do not think about the people who were native to the lands that we now live upon. Sometimes the land was less than honorably, if not forcibly, taken from them. Those who lived on the land where we now reside are connected to us as ancestors of place.

Today, research the identity of the native peoples of the land where you currently live. Take a few moments in meditation, sitting outside directly upon the land if possible, to consider the chain of events that possibly took place to result in your home being upon that land today. How can you honor those who came before you and were native to the land?

Blake Octavian Blair

 March 27
Saturday

2nd ♏

☽ v/c 7:48 pm

Color of the Day: Indigo
Incense of the Day: Sage

Passover begins at sundown

Seed Catalog Spell

It's time to dream of summer and plan a magical garden. The soil is still cold, but the latest seed catalogs are out and you can always dream.

Cast a circle, calling in the Goddess:

By the earth that is her body, the air that is her breath, the fire of her strong spirit, and the waters of her living womb, I cast this circle.

I call what is above and what is below, and ask them to unite—earth and sunlight—to grow my magical garden.

In sacred space, contemplate your own garden and which herbs and flowers you could seed and grow to use in your magical practice. Focused on love spells? Grow roses and basil. Interested in joy and happiness? Plant calendula and sunflowers. Practicing protection? Plant garlic and rosemary.

Once you have envisioned your magical garden, thank the directions and open the circle, ready now to order from those seed catalogs.

Dallas Jennifer Cobb

March 28
Sunday

2nd ♍

☽ → ♎ 1:22 am

Full Moon 2:48 pm

Color of the Day: Amber
Incense of the Day: Hyacinth

Palm Sunday

home Protection

This is a favorable time to cast spells of protection. Here is one that uses the four magical elements: air, fire, water, and earth. You will need a stick of incense, a burner, a lighter, sea salt, water, a bowl, and a fan. It is easier to do this spell with two people, but it can be done alone.

First put the incense in the burner and safely light it. This represents air and fire. Next put the water in the bowl and add a pinch of sea salt. This represents water and earth. If you have two people, you can bless the rooms one at a time, first with incense and then with salt water. By yourself, it may be easier to do the whole home with incense and then with salt water. Fan the smoke so it touches all parts of your home. Sprinkle salt water on the walls, floors, and ceilings. Draw a pentacle in salt water over every door, window, and other opening such as vents or electrical outlets. When finished, be sure to extinguish the incense.

Elizabeth Barrette

NOTES:

March 29
Monday

3rd ♎

☽ v/c 8:08 pm

Color of the Day: Ivory
Incense of the Day: Hyssop

healthy Pet Magic

We all love our pets. These animals who bless our lives are true friends, and they depend on us to keep them healthy. So in addition to taking the best possible care of your fur baby (or scale baby), it doesn't hurt to work a little magic into their maintenance.

Think about a symbol that represents general good health to you, perhaps a plump red heart to represent vigor, a bone for strength, or a sun for vitality. Draw the symbol on your pet's belongings and recite:

Good health, long life, and lots of love.

Here are some ways to use your symbol:

- Draw it on a food container, such as bag of dog or cat kibble or a canister of fish food.

- Trace it onto treats and toys with your finger.

- Paint it on their bed or stitch it into the corner of a favored blanket.

- Dip your finger into their water bowl and draw the symbol.

- Draw it on a slip of paper and place it near their enclosure.

- Paint it on the underside of their food bowl.

Kate Freuler

NOTES:

March 30
Tuesday

3rd ♎

☽ → ♏ 1:33 am

Color of the Day: Black
Incense of the Day: Ylang-ylang

A Spell for a Speedy Workweek

If you work a nine-to-five job, Monday though Friday, Tuesdays can be tough. The barrage of Monday is over, but it feels like you're an eternity away from Friday! To make your workweek fly by and ensure that you still get all of your essential tasks done, try this.

Use a small jar or bowl to dilute five drops of pure peppermint oil with twenty drops of carrier oil. (Olive oil is fine, but you may also use jojoba oil, safflower oil, or almond oil.) Before you go to work, anoint a tumbled piece of bloodstone with the oil and say:

My day flies by, easily and with success.
Tomorrow is as good as Friday.

Carry the anointed stone against your skin. You may place a piece of flannel or linen between your clothes and the stone to prevent staining. Know that your day will be a success and that it will pass quickly and easily.

Thorn Mooney

 ## March 31
Wednesday

3rd ♏

☽ v/c 8:29 pm

Color of the Day: Gray
Incense of the Day: Bay laurel

Healing and Connecting with Trees

Spring is a time of renewal and rebirth. Connecting with the essence and energy of trees is healing and can be done at any time of the year. Whenever you need to become more grounded with nature, perform this simple tree magick.

Find a tree that you adore and can connect with. Place your arms around the tree trunk and hug it, placing the side of your face on the bark. Close your eyes and take a deep breath. Concentrate on what you can see in your third eye. Don't worry if you don't see anything at first. It may take some practice. As you connect with the energy of the tree, ask the tree to ground you and heal whatever pain you are dealing with. Send the pain into the tree and visualize it going down deep into the earth. Say these words:

I give gratitude and thanks
to this tree for this healing
connection that grounds me.

Repeat these words until you feel a deep connection.

Sapphire Moonbeam

April

This month we move from dark to light, from cold to warm, from brown to green. April is a magical month that starts with April Fools' Day and ends on the eve of May Day, begins with a joke and ends with an outdoor sleep-out. Here in Ontario, Canada, the average temperature at the beginning of April is close to freezing. It's common to have snow on the ground. Throughout April a magical transformation occurs: the temperature climbs as high as 66 degrees Fahrenheit (19 degrees Celsius) and flowers bloom.

Post-equinox, the days grow longer. Between April 1 and 30, the daylight increases from 12 hours and 46 minutes to 14 hours and 8 minutes. As the sun travels northward, it climbs in the sky. Not only do days lengthen, but shadows shorten as well. It is inviting to get outdoors. Like the plants that need sunlight to conduct photosynthesis, we humans need sunlight to help manufacture vitamin D.

This month, make time to enjoy the outdoors. Get out in the daylight, take evening walks in the twilight after dinner, contemplate your garden, and turn your face toward the sun at every chance. With winter coming to an end, now is your time to transform.

Dallas Jennifer Cobb

April 1
Thursday

3rd ♏

☽ → ♐ 1:59 am

Color of the Day: Green
Incense of the Day: Nutmeg

April Fools' Day – All Fools' Day

"Don't Be Fooled" Affirmation

In honor of April Fools' Day, here's an affirmation to guard against falling for illusions and being tricked. Light a white candle in a clear glass container and place it on a small mirror. Gaze upon the candle and chant:

I can read between the lines.

I can see what isn't shown.

I will not be tricked or fooled.

I will learn what isn't known.

Allow the candle to burn out safely. Carry the mirror with you.

Ember Grant

April 2
Friday

3rd ♐

Color of the Day: White
Incense of the Day: Vanilla

Good Friday

Squirrel Power!

Yes, they may be cute and playful, but squirrels are also keen gatherers that can teach us much about planning for the future and building abundance. To connect with the squirrel as a type of spirit animal, it is a good idea to take time to feed your local squirrels. In the springtime they are usually relegated to different types of grasses since vegetables and nuts are hard to come by this time of year. Good things to feed them are raw, cut-up vegetables such as yellow squash, broccoli, and peas. They can also have some fruits, like watermelon and grapes, in small amounts. Dedicate a small squirrel feeder to the intention of building a spiritual relationship with their realm, and keep a small squirrel figurine on your altar to call in their energy.

Michael Furie

April 3
Saturday

3rd ♐

☽ v/c 1:24 am

☽ → ♑ 4:13 am

Color of the Day: Black
Incense of the Day: Pine

Passover ends

Nature Divination

Augury is an ancient form of divination. Simplified, it's the act of asking a question and then observing the behavior of nature to get an answer.

Go to a place with wildlife, such as a park or other natural area. Find a quiet spot to sit down comfortably, preferably away from other people. Close your eyes and ask your question. When you open your eyes, sit and watch for a while. What animals do you see, and how are they behaving? Birds in a loud flock represent upheaval and travel, while a single bird singing loudly signals a message. A squirrel gathering food indicates that you need to start preparing for change. Even insects are important: if a fly keeps annoying you by landing on your face, your situation requires immediate action.

Also pay attention to the weather. Did a cloud suddenly block out the sun? Did the wind pick up suddenly and give you a chill? Both of those things are a warning.

The more you practice this, the more you will come to understand nature's messages.

Kate Freuler

NOTES:

April 4
Sunday

3rd ♑

4th Quarter 6:02 am

Color of the Day: Amber
Incense of the Day: Eucalyptus

Easter

Eggs of hidden Blessings

Easter is such a Pagan holiday. With its abundance of pre-Christian fertility symbolism, it celebrates the renewal of life and spring. Eggs represent life, and utilizing those brightly colored ones from childhood in our magical work is a great way that we as Witches can reconnect to those cultural elements on our own terms.

You will need several white hard-boiled eggs, a commercial egg-dyeing kit, and a white crayon.

Begin by designing sigils for various blessings, such as health, prosperity, love, etc. If you need help, Laura Tempest Zakroff's *Sigil Witchery* is an eggcellent resource. (Sorry, I couldn't resist!) Draw these symbols on the eggs with the crayon, contemplating their meanings.

Follow the instructions on your dye kit. While the eggs soak, say:

Cosmic egg of all creation,

Be present in your symbol here.

Alive here now with exaltation,

Hidden blessings now appear!

The sigils will remain white, revealing their magical intention. Hide or eat the eggs. Bon appétit!

Storm Faerywolf

Notes:

April 5
Monday

4th ♑

☽ v/c 3:05 am

☽ → ♒ 9:04 am

Color of the Day: Silver
Incense of the Day: Rosemary

Dandelion Perspective Spell

April 5 is National Dandelion Day in the US. Dandelions are viewed by some as weeds, but a weed is simply an unloved flower. This spell will help with balance, power, and a change of perspective.

Gather up dandelions for your altar or sacred space. Place stones and crystals around the flowers in a circle. Use yellow calcite for positive energy and yellow jasper for balance, and add clear quartz crystals to amplify your magical intentions. Chant these words at least three times:

Bring me a perspective that is new.
Help me change my point of view.

I seek balance and I seek power. Allow me to grow like this beautiful flower.

Keeping an open mind is best for me. I am grateful for your guidance. Blessed be!

Offer the dandelion flowers at the base of your favorite tree in gratitude to the Earth Mother for her endless wisdom and bountiful gifts.

Sapphire Moonbeam

 ## April 6
Tuesday

4th ♒

Color of the Day: Maroon
Incense of the Day: Bayberry

Blow Out the Old

Spring is finally in the air, both literally and figuratively. If you open your window, you can probably smell a new freshness and hear the birds changing from their winter songs to the ones they sing in the spring. Depending on where you live, there may be the scent of flowers growing. Even in the city, the air will smell cleaner and you will sense the potential for growth and new beginnings. Throw open a window—or all of them—and use a small hand fan or scarf to waft the air over you. As you do so, say:

Spring air, so fresh and clean,

Blow away the cobwebs of winter.

Clear my mind and spirit.

Bring in your energy for new growth

And the potential for positive change.

Thank you, air, for all
you carry with you

And for all you carry away!

Blessed be, O power of air.

Deborah Blake

April 7
Wednesday

4th ≈

☽ v/c 6:05 am

☽ → ♓ 4:30 pm

Color of the Day: White
Incense of the Day: Marjoram

Inspiration Incense and Charm

Mercury, ruler of the mind and communication, is currently moving through Aries, the bringer of new beginnings and a can-do attitude. This pairing is auspicious for those of us who are engaged in the arts, as it can help us tune in to our muses and break through creative blocks.

Begin by making the following incense recipe:

- 1 tablespoon ground sandalwood

- 1 tablespoon ground rosemary

- 1 tablespoon ground copal

As you burn the incense over charcoal, say the following charm:

Spirits of inspiration, I conjure thee.

Be here now; reveal yourself to me.

Open the doorway and
unblock the mind.

You have the key to what I need to find.

Devin Hunter

April 8
Thursday

4th ♓

Color of the Day: Crimson
Incense of the Day: Jasmine

Cultivating Tradition

Today in Japan, Hana-Matsuri is celebrated. A combined celebration of spring , traditional Japanese culture, and quite possibly Buddha's birthday, the festivities are abundant and gorgeous. Imagine lots of flowers, costumes, and kimonos! Today, perform your own "cultivating tradition" spell.

Choose some small icons that represent your cultural, religious, and familial traditions. My origins are in England, Scotland, and Ireland. Easy associations are tea, shortbread cookies, and my Claddagh ring— a traditional Irish symbol of love, loyalty, and friendship.

Place your cultural icons on your altar. Dress in traditional garb or wear jewelry handed down through your lineage. Safely light a candle to illuminate and warm your traditions. Make a traditional drink or food, and as you sip or nibble, know that your traditions live on within you. As you pay sacred homage to your traditional roots and ancestry, know that they enrich your life and community.

Be sure to extinguish the candle.

Dallas Jennifer Cobb

April 9
Friday

4th ♓

☽ v/c 7:48 pm

Color of the Day: Rose
Incense of the Day: Violet

Moving the Rain

Spring brings rain in many parts of the world. Sometimes this is welcome, and other times not. Too much rain can cause flooding, while other parts of the land get none. Here is a spell to send unwanted rain where it is needed more.

Gather these items:

• A large map of your continent

• Several small containers, such as shot glasses or bowls, one bigger than the others

• Some water (rainwater if possible)

Check the weather conditions on your continent to find out where it is wet and where it is dry right now. Place the map on your altar, then put the big container over where you live and the smaller ones over locations where there currently is also rain. Visualize the current rainy weather in your location. Then say:

We give thanks for the rain, but others need it more. Please give our rain to (name of dry area).

Pick up the big container and move it to that part of the map. Visualize the rain in your location moving to that dry location. (The smaller containers remain in place, since you are not trying to move that rain.) Then you can clean up the altar.

Elizabeth Barrette

NOTES:

April 10
Saturday

4th ♓
☽ → ♈ 2:11 am

Color of the Day: Blue
Incense of the Day: Magnolia

Earth healing on Arbor Day

On this date in 1872, the first Arbor Day was celebrated in Nebraska. This is a perfectly pagan holiday, as it was created to promote the planting of trees. I can't think of a more perfectly aligned holiday for earth-based spiritualities!

Today, either plant a tree or pot or repot a houseplant, and if you're able, make a donation (even a small one) to a tree or other environmental conservation organization. During any of these activities, hold the intention that the growth of the tree or plant you planted carry your magical intent of healing the planet as it grows. See the tree's green glowing light gently wrap around the planet as its roots grow deeper and its branches grow taller. As the green light spreads, hold the intention that other people will also have the realization that trees and the earth are vital to preserve.

Blake Octavian Blair

April 11
Sunday

4th ♈
New Moon 10:31 pm

Color of the Day: Yellow
Incense of the Day: Almond

New Moon Blessing Ritual

She goes away. We're forced to wait and believe that she will return. We cannot see her with our physical eyes, yet we know she remains in her orbit high above the earth. It is us who must wait for her return.

A new moon calls upon us to have faith. It signals a time of new beginnings. For this spell you will need a black candle, a fireproof candle holder, a saucer, and salt.

Place your black candle in the holder, then set it upon the saucer. Pour a circle of salt around the base of the candle. Light the candle and say:

Though darkness surrounds me, I am filled with light. I trust in the universe on this moonless night. I await new beginnings and new opportunities.

Allow the candle to safely burn out. Place the salt on your altar.

Najah Lightfoot

April 12
Monday

1st ♈

☽ v/c 8:06 am

☽ → ♉ 1:44 pm

Color of the Day: Gray
Incense of the Day: Clary sage

Ramadan begins at sundown

Aries Moon Spell for Motivation

The Aries new moon from last night is still in effect for the first part of today, which provides magical folks with a double shot of oomph to apply to workings pertaining to new beginnings. Aries is the first sign of the zodiac and is characterized by spontaneity, impulsiveness, excitement, and an unflagging desire to triumph in the face of obstacles. Meanwhile, the new moon is an ideal time to work toward new goals and to draw things to you. With the power of the new moon in Aries, any task you set your mind on today is that much more likely to succeed!

To use the energy of the Aries new moon, carve your name into a red candle. If you have a specific goal in mind, you may state it aloud now, or carve a symbol that represents that goal for you into the candle, alongside your name. If you don't have a specific goal in mind, that's okay. This spell will generally draw motivating, success-oriented energy to you. Safely burn this candle throughout the day.

It's okay to snuff it out and relight it as needed. Just don't leave an unattended candle burning!

Thorn Mooney

NOTES:

April 13
Tuesday

1st ♉

Color of the Day: Red
Incense of the Day: Cinnamon

Fortunetelling with Scrabble

There are many ways of predicting the future. Scrabble tiles may be one of the most inventive and fun methods of all. Ask a question, throw the tiles, and see what words come up (if any). Or play a game of Scrabble with the direct and stated intention of receiving an answer or information. Always be prepared to accept an answer that is different from what you expected or perhaps even the opposite of what you'd hoped for. And remember that no answer *is* an answer. It may be a sign that there is no need for you to know just yet, or the universe is not ready to divulge that information, or it may not be your right to know.

Prior to any spell, it is wise to call upon a higher power for guidance:

A glimpse of the future I seek. Please, friendly forces, give us a peek.

This request is offered with a light heart, accepting your answer in whole or in part.

Emyme

April 14
Wednesday

1st ♉

☽ v/c 8:00 pm

Color of the Day: Topaz
Incense of the Day: Lilac

Rainbow Flags

There has never been a more important time to embrace diversity and honor the spectrum of color that life offers to us. Crafting is a fun way to bring a sense of pride and compassion into the home. Cut twenty-two triangles from rainbow fabric and stitch them onto eight feet of cord, spacing them equally apart.

As you stitch, say the following prayer of unity eight times:

Light includes all seven colors, a continuum clear. In every triangle prism, drop of water, or tear, we invoke the diversity we celebrate here.

All are welcome as a spectrum of love; A rainbow is a reflection, as blessed below as it is above!

When done, seal the energy by tying the ends of the rope to make a figure-eight knot on each end. Hang this in your entryway to proudly display the spectrum celebrating free will and self-identity. Take PRIDE in birthdays, mitzvahs, barbeques, and anything else!

Estha McNevin

April 15
Thursday

1st ♉

☽ → ♊ 2:35 am

Color of the Day: Turquoise
Incense of the Day: Apricot

An April Rain Spell

April rains are cleansing and nourishing. They cleanse the earth and enable seeds to sprout and buds to swell toward maturity. April rain can also cleanse and charge scrying tools such as magic mirrors or crystal balls. To do this, select a rainy April morning. Place your scrying tool outside in a safe place, such as in a window box or beneath a shrub. Let it stay out for about an hour, then bring it in and, if needed, rinse it quickly in water. Dry it with a clean white cotton towel. Then hold your scrying tool and say:

The April rain has left you clean.

Now you're surrounded with energy calm and serene.

Please be ready to help me with my magical tasks,

Such as seeing into the future, present, or past.

Your scrying tool is now cleansed, charged, and ready to use.

James Kambos

April 16
Friday

1st ♊

Color of the Day: Purple
Incense of the Day: Thyme

Fairy Luck Spell

April 16 is the Day of the Mushroom. In European cultures mushrooms are considered a symbol of hope and good luck. Mushrooms are surrounded by fairy energy. When you find a mushroom, know that the fairies knew they could trust you with their presence nearby. Cup your hands around the sides of the mushroom without touching it. In order to promote good luck and encourage more of it to enter your life, say these words:

On this day I thank the fae.

I accept the good luck and blessings they send my way!

You can utilize this spell at any time later on by envisioning a lucky mushroom in your third eye and repeating these words.

Sapphire Moonbeam

♌ April 17
Saturday

1st ♊

☽ v/c 11:03 am

☽ → ♋ 3:25 pm

Color of the Day: Brown
Incense of the Day: Sage

Peaceful Trails Water

On a sunny, calm day, collect a jar of water from a tranquil pond, lake, or fountain. As you do so, spend a moment feeling how still and serene the place is. Notice the gentle ripples in the water, the soothing lapping sounds, and the harmonious existence of any wildlife. Imagine that calmness and serenity infusing the jar of water like a soft ray of sunshine. Put the lid on the jar and take it home.

Dribble a trail of this water on the sidewalk or street outside your home, then up the driveway, front path, or hallway, all the way to your front door. Anyone who enters your space will be cleansed by the vibration of the calming water and bring only peaceful energy with them into your home.

You can also use this water to attract serenity in other ways, such as watering your potted plants with it or adding a drop to your bath.

Kate Freuler

♌ April 18
Sunday

1st ♋

Color of the Day: Orange
Incense of the Day: Hyacinth

Peaceful home Carpet Powder

This simple spell is designed to dispel negative or stagnant energies and to bless your home with a sense of peace and balance. Lavender has long been known for its properties of bringing calm, peace, and balance.

Gather the following materials:

• A blue candle

• A mixing bowl

• Baking soda

• Dried lavender flowers

• Some salt

• A vacuum

Light the blue candle. In the bowl, mix together the baking soda and lavender flowers. Focus on the feelings of balance and calm that you wish to instill in your space. Add a small bit of salt and mix well.

Sprinkle this mixture on your carpets throughout your house. As you do so, repeat:

Evil, be gone,

Balance restored.

Once you have finished, allow the mixture to sit for about 10-15 minutes, then vacuum it up. Allow the candle to finish burning down safely.

Storm Faerywolf

NOTES:

April 19
Monday

1st ♐ ♋

☉ → ♉ 4:33 pm

☽ v/c 8:03 pm

Color of the Day: White
Incense of the Day: Lily

Spell for a Rainy Day

Take advantage of April showers with this spell that uses rain and the element of water. All you need to do is go outside on a rainy day, visualize your goal, and chant the following:

Rain is falling to the ground.

Water bring your magic down.

With every drop that you allow,

Fulfill the wish I whisper now.

State your goal.

Ember Grant

 ## April 20
Tuesday

1st ♋

☽ → ♌ 2:11 am

2nd Quarter 2:59 am

Color of the Day: Black
Incense of the Day: Ginger

Cleansing with Spring herbs

One of the joys of spring is the coming of the first fresh herbs to gardens and markets. Some may even sprout in your own yard. It is probably no accident that many of the earliest herbs are especially good at detoxifying the body. Back in the old days, a winter diet was mostly made up of preserved or fresh meat and whatever vegetables could be stored for a long time. By the time people made it to spring, they needed all the cleansing they could get.

These days, our winter diets might be better, but our spirits can undoubtedly use a boost come spring. Try using some fresh spring herbs in your magical work. You can also make a healing tea from fresh (edible) herbs like peppermint or lemon balm. Bless the herb on your altar first to give it an extra boost, and say:

May this fresh spring herb
bring its healing and refreshing
qualities to my body and spirit.

Then sip it slowly and mindfully.

Deborah Blake

 ## April 21
Wednesday

2nd ♌

Color of the Day: Yellow
Incense of the Day: Honeysuckle

Overlook It Spell

Happy Taurus season! The sun recently moved into Taurus, ushering in a time of hard work, beauty, and home-centered thinking. Taurus is one of those signs that likes to have everything in place, and presentation matters! Unfortunately, things can't be perfect all the time, so here is a spell to get people to overlook unsightly things that might mar your presentation. (This works great for when in-laws or parents visit.)

Take a foot of pink ribbon and empower it by saying the following charm:

Everything is perfect, everything is fine,

Not a hair out of place or error to find.

Overlook them and forget what you see.

You won't have one complaint
when it comes to me.

Now tie the ribbon to your left wrist or ankle, making a bow with the remaining ribbon. Leave it on while that person is near and remove it when you no longer need it.

Devin hunter

April 22
Thursday

2nd ♌

☽ v/c 8:05 am

☽ → ♍ 9:08 am

Color of the Day: Purple
Incense of the Day: Balsam

Earth Day

Earthing/Grounding

It's Earth Day, so let's practice earthing, or grounding—attuning our energy with that of the earth.

Stress, pollution, illness, and negativity can create free radicals: molecules that have lost one or more electrons. Free radicals can induce oxidative stress, which can lead to diabetes, cardiovascular disease, and multiple sclerosis.

Good ions are oxygen atoms with extra negatively-charged electrons. Abundant in nature, they're present in the earth, beach, mountains, and water. Negative ions neutralize free radicals, promote healing, and balance the autonomic nervous system. The earth has the capacity to restore health and balance in the human body.

Today, go outside and sit where you can place your bare feet on the ground. Sit quietly for half an hour. Be aware of the subtle shift in your energy as your body attunes to the resonant energy of the earth. You are now grounded.

Dallas Jennifer Cobb

 April 23
Friday

2nd ♍

Color of the Day: Coral
Incense of the Day: Rose

Spell to Ease Work Stress

No matter how enjoyable a job may be, there are still times of difficulty and stress. This spell can help during those rough patches.

As soon as you have a quiet moment at work, even if it's in the bathroom, close your eyes and envision yourself surrounded by an orb of electric-blue light. Within this orb you are protected from the chaos of work stress. Not only does this orb protect you from future stress, but it also is spiritually magnetic. Feel it pulling the harmful energy out of your body and transforming it into more electric-blue power to strengthen itself. Feel all the stress leave you and become a beneficial part of your new shield.

When you're ready, open your eyes and return to work with the knowledge that any stress sent your way will be blocked and absorbed by your shield, protecting you from all chaos and harm.

Michael Furie

April 24
Saturday

2nd ♍

☽ v/c 6:50 am

☽ → ♎ 12:06 pm

Color of the Day: Indigo
Incense of the Day: Ivy

herbal Smudge home Cleanse

Saturdays, which are under the rule of Saturn, are a wonderful time to do some hearth and home magic. Let's take this opportunity to do a bit of energetic clearing using an herb that is also associated with Saturday's energetic currents: mullein. Mullein is known for keeping away evil and malevolent energies—perfect for upping your household protection against stray, unwanted vibes!

Gather a heatproof and fireproof vessel, an incense charcoal, and a couple spoonfuls of mullein. Get the charcoal lit and burning, and add some mullein on top. As it smokes, work your way around your home counterclockwise while wafting the smoke. Recite an incantation such as this:

By power of mullein, clean and cleanse.

By power of fire and earth, smoke and herb, my home I defend.

My home is a sanctuary that shall not upend.

Blessed be.

Blake Octavian Blair

April 25
Sunday

2nd ♎

Color of the Day: Gold
Incense of the Day: Frankincense

Under the Creative Moon

With the full moon tomorrow, this is a great time for some creative kitchen witchery. Collect all of your bowls, cookie sheets, cake pans, measuring cups—everything. Wash it all and set aside whatever you no longer use. Round up every recipe you can find, then update and organize them in one place. Go through your pantry and ruthlessly discard out-of-date items. Tomorrow, drop off items no longer needed at your local thrift store, then purchase fresh supplies and new tools.

Plan for a time of blessing your loved ones with nourishment, sharing recipes, and teaching the next generation the magic of creating food with love.

Emyme

April 26
Monday

2nd ♎

☽ v/c 8:40 am

☽ → ♏ 12:18 pm

Full Moon 11:32 pm

Color of the Day: Ivory
Incense of the Day: Narcissus

Daytime Full Moon
Tool Consecration

The full moon is a great time to cleanse and consecrate magical tools. Many people will place crystals, oils, herbs, and other magical accoutrements in the light of the moon to absorb its energy, but the truth is that full moon energy is present during the daylight hours, too.

Use today to inventory your magical tools, dismantling those that no longer serve you or giving away those that may find better homes with others. You should regularly charge and reaffirm those that you decide to keep or that you've only recently acquired. Choose a favorite magical oil, if you have one, or simply use plain olive oil or magically consecrated water. Anoint each tool by dabbing it and saying:

*I cleanse, consecrate, and empower
this (tool) so that it may serve
me in my work. So mote it be.*

Allow your tools to sit in view of the sky over the course of the day, no matter the weather. Be careful with your colored quartz crystals, such as amethyst, as sunlight can cause them to fade over time.

Thorn Mooney

NOTES:

April 27
Tuesday

3rd ♏

Color of the Day: Scarlet
Incense of the Day: Ylang-ylang

Keep Your Side of the Street Clean

On a regular basis we have experiences that frustrate or annoy us. And in between those times there are moments when life shows us that we are not in control. During those times, I'm reminded of the old adage "Keep your side of the street clean."

For this spell you will need a small container, some water, and a broom.

Fill the container with water. Hold it in your hands and say:

Blessed be, element of water; water that cleanses, renews, and refreshes.

Dip your fingers in the water and sprinkle a few drops on your broom. Say:

Blessed be, this broom, which sweeps away that which no longer serves me.

Pour the water onto your doorstep. Sweep the doorstep from side to side. As you sweep, let go of things you cannot control, and know that sometimes the best thing you can do is keep your side of the street clean.

Najah Lightfoot

April 28
Wednesday

3rd ♏

☽ v/c 8:31 am

☽ → ♐ 11:42 am

Color of the Day: Brown
Incense of the Day: Lavender

Floralia Celebration

Floralia was an ancient Roman festival that was held from April 28 to May 3. It honored Flora, the goddess of flowers. People hosted games and theatrical performances.

You can celebrate Floralia alone or with your coven. Plant summer flowers such as daylilies, clematis, sunflowers, or zinnias to honor the goddess. Planting peas or beans—especially sweet peas, grown for their fragrant blooms—promotes fertility. Pick spring flowers like tulips and daffodils to make flower crowns, boutonnières, or wrist corsages. Play games related to blossoms or gardening, such as the card game Lotus, the dice game Bloom, or the board game The Little Flower Shop. A favorite form of divination is to pick flowers, determine a meaning for each one, and blow them across a pool of water. The first to reach the far side indicates the answer to your question.

Elizabeth Barrette

April 29
Thursday

3rd ♐

Color of the Day: White
Incense of the Day: Mulberry

Feed the Birds and Welcome Spring!

Tuppence charms date back to Victorian times and involve binding a coin with ribbon and seeds, then hanging it in a tree for the birds to nibble loose. This luck-casting utilizes the cycle of nature and the fertility of birds to imbue the charm with magick. Picking exotic coins is best. Later, a treasure hunt for these coins can be had, giving this spell an extra aura of luck and chance.

Gather the following:

- 1 cup honey
- 1 cup cooked rice
- ½ cup apple juice
- 3 cage-free eggs
- ½ cup meringue powder
- 12–16 ounces regional seed mix
- 12 coins bound up with green ribbon
- 12 silicon cupcake molds

Mix the first six ingredients together with your hands, then pack around each coin and ribbon. Press into a silicone cupcake mold. Leave a bit of ribbon dangling out for hanging later.

Dry them in the oven at 190 degrees F. for three hours. When set, hang the charms in the trees around your yard.

Estha McNevin

NOTES:

April 30
Friday

3rd ♐

☽ v/c 9:27 am

☽ → ♑ 12:16 pm

Color of the Day: Pink
Incense of the Day: Mint

A Cleansing Spell

In some regions of Europe centuries ago, this date was considered to be the official end of winter. Cleansing rituals were performed to purify homes, farms, and livestock in preparation for a fruitful growing season. Many rituals involved fire. Bonfires were set, or sometimes straw brooms were set afire. These fires were meant to burn away the last remnants of winter and cleanse the environment. This spell is based on these ancient traditions. Use it to cleanse your living space or to bring good fortune. Begin by selecting three straws from a broom. Ignite them. Let them burn or smolder until they're ash in a fireplace or heatproof container. As they burn, say:

I dedicate this fire to the earth and sun,

And to the summer season still to come.

Let bounty spread across the land.

I send this wish from my own hand.

When the ashes have cooled, sprinkle them as a blessing in a favorite outdoor area.

James Kambos

NOTES:

May

Welcome to the famously merry month of May! Though it was originally named after the Greek fertility goddess Maia, the Catholic Church has since designated this month as sacred to the Virgin Mary, even referring to her as "the Queen of May" during this time. Day one of this flower-filled month is the beloved holiday of Beltane, during which the veil that usually conceals the world of the fairies fades, and our power to make contact with them reaches its yearly peak. Indeed, May's birth flower is a fairy favorite: the lily of the valley. As for our skies, this month they host the Eta Aquariids meteor shower, which reaches its peak around May 6 and is most visible before the sunrise.

May is also the month when the light half of the year begins to assert itself in earnest, and we sense the days lengthening, the sun growing warmer, and the leaves filling out the trees. This allows us to gaze bravely into our own brilliance and to courageously release anything that has been holding us back from being our most radiant, expansive, beautiful selves. Indeed, May's bright presence reminds us to claim the vital prosperity that is our birthright and our natural state.

Tess Whitehurst

 # May 1
Saturday

3rd ♑

Color of the Day: Blue
Incense of the Day: Sandalwood

Beltane

Love Is Blooming

Today is Beltane, otherwise known as May Day. It celebrates the union of the Goddess and the God, fertility, abundance, and of course love. Traditionally it is often seen as a holiday that is raucous and sensual—and certainly it can be. But love takes many forms, and Beltane is the perfect time to focus on whichever kind or kinds of love you wish to invite into your life. This can include romantic or sexual love, but also the love of family, friends, pets, community, or anything else that will fill your heart with joy. Beltane is a fire holiday, so if you can, light a bonfire and dance around it. (If you can't have a bonfire, light a red candle in a cauldron or firesafe bowl instead. Snuff it out when you are done.) As you dance, say or chant:

Beltane fires,

Sacred and wild,

Bring me love,

Both sweet and mild;

The kind of love

I need and desire.

Come to me

With Beltane's fire.

Deborah Blake

NOTES:

May 2
Sunday

3rd ♑

☽ v/c 10:38 am

☽ → ♒ 3:31 pm

Color of the Day: Yellow
Incense of the Day: Eucalyptus

Mindful Magick

The practice of mindfulness has gained quite a foothold in recent years. It seems everyone from elders to children is practicing mindful meditation. We all need ways to calm our mind and release stress.

For our spell today, we are going to practice being mindful magickal practitioners. Find a stone, crystal, leaf, feather, or flower that grabs your attention. Go to a location where you will not be disturbed. Hold your item in your hand and gaze at it lovingly. Slow your breathing. When you begin to relax, close your eyes. Feel the item with your fingers. Try to quiet your thoughts, and allow the item to speak its magick to you.

When you feel ready, open your eyes. Thank your item for being with you. Return your item to Mother Earth, or place it on your altar, where it will help you to remember to be mindful.

Najah Lightfoot

May 3
Monday

3rd ♒

4th Quarter 3:50 pm

Color of the Day: Lavender
Incense of the Day: Neroli

Pressing Flowers

Collect flower petals to save for use in future rituals and for decorating your magical journals. If you use cut flowers as altar decorations, this is a great way to preserve some of that energy for later use.

To press flowers, you need only a few pieces of white paper or paper towels and the largest, heaviest book you can find. On a piece of paper or paper towel, lay the petals you wish to press. Do not allow them to touch or overlap. When they are all arranged, put a second sheet on top of them, sandwiching them. The paper will absorb the plant fluids over time. Place the whole thing between the central pages of the book. You may place other heavy items on top of the book. Allow to sit for several days. When the petals are dry and flattened, they can be inserted or glued into your book of shadows or used in other magical work.

Thorn Mooney

May 4
Tuesday

4th ♒

☽ v/c 8:05 pm

☽ → ♓ 10:09 pm

Color of the Day: Red

Incense of the Day: Basil

A Cushion Beloved

Love is in the air. Today, spend time with a partner and cast magick together for the future you both are working to manifest. Love pillows are a stylish and creative way to experiment with more sexual positions while casting fertility and relationship magick together as a couple.

Using one yard of a silk brocade fabric, cut two large circles, each thirty-six inches wide. Blind-stitch them together and fill with any of the following components to create a manifestation spell. Use this pillow during intimate moments to bring joy and fulfillment to your many needs and shared goals.

- 8 cups buckwheat
- 8 cups rainbow corn kernels
- 8 cups rice
- 1 couple's photo
- 7 cups rose petals
- 7 drops essential rose oil
- 7 drops essential saffron oil
- 7 drops essential agar oil
- Images or small objects that signify your needs
- Items of worth, value, or sentiment
- Hair from each partner
- Cottonwood tree seed fluff

Estha McNevin

NOTES:

May 5
Wednesday

4th ♓

Color of the Day: Topaz
Incense of the Day: Marjoram

Cinco de Mayo

Celebrate Cultural Diversity

Today is Cinco de Mayo, the day commemorating the Mexican army's victory over the French at the Battle of Puebla in 1862. In the United States, the holiday has become one of celebrating Mexican-American culture.

It is very easy to form misconceptions about other cultures due to misinformation or a lack of knowledge. Today, celebrate cultural diversity by learning a bit more about Mexican-American culture. Perhaps listen to some traditional Mexican music and learn about the artist, or find a cookbook of traditional Mexican recipes and try your hand at making one. While you undertake your adventure in learning, safely light a yellow candle on your altar in an act of summoning inspiration and knowledge. As you light it, say the following simple enchantment:

Candle burning bright, illuminate the beauty of diversity this day and night!

Be sure to extinguish the candle.

Blake Octavian Blair

May 6
Thursday

4♄ ♓

Color of the Day: Purple
Incense of the Day: Nutmeg

A Faery Garden Offering Spell

Making regular offerings to the local fae spirits is a good way for a Witch to further develop their power and sensitivity. For this spell you will need the following materials:

- Crystals, jewelry, and other beautiful shiny objects

- A small bowl

- A small cup or glass

- Some food for an offering (such as fruit, bread, or honey)

- Some beverage for an offering (whiskey is traditional)

Ideally this spell should be done outside in your garden. If this is not possible, you will need to obtain a houseplant for this purpose. Choose an area of your yard (or in the soil of the houseplant) and arrange the beautiful objects in a manner that is pleasing. Include the bowl and the cup or glass.

Place your offerings of food and beverage in the bowl and cup. Say:

To the fae I freely give
This humble offering.

May my sight be awakened to the land,

And may there ever be peace between us.

Dispose of any food offerings after twenty-four hours. Repeat this spell as often as you are inspired to do so. I suggest at least weekly!

Storm Faerywolf

NOTES:

May 7
Friday

4♄ ♓

☽ v/c 3:36 am

☽ → ♈ 7:52 am

Color of the Day: Rose
Incense of the Day: Orchid

Hecate Justice Spell

This spell isn't meant to be used for vengeful or frivolous purposes but rather as a final resort, since it not only asks a powerful deity for help but also seeks to neutralize harm caused by the wrongdoer.

To begin, place three unlit white candles on an altar table around an image of Hecate (or three keys) and a bulb of garlic. Close your eyes and meditate on Hecate until you can feel her presence. When you feel her near, safely light the candles in her honor and plead your case. Tell her why you need her help. Don't declare what type of justice you wish to befall the wrongdoer; that's her decision. Simply tell her what happened and then recite this spell:

With thanks and honor, I ask this gift, from my life this burden lift.

Goddess Hecate, I implore, unto (wrongdoer's name) balance restore.

Make your justice swift and true, and their treachery please undo.

Extinguish the candles and bury the garlic.

Michael Furie

NOTES:

May 8
Saturday

4th ♈

Color of the Day: Gray
Incense of the Day: Patchouli

Bless This Vessel

I drive less in the winter because of the hazards of the road. But with spring now fully in blossom and the snow finally gone, it's time to start journeying again.

Before you travel, take time to bless your vehicle, bless the journey, and bless the inhabitants of your vehicle. Whether the vehicle is a car, truck, motorcycle, boat, canoe, kayak, or bicycle, use this blessing before departing.

Lay your hands upon the vehicle and say:

I bless this vessel with love and light,

*That she may carry us
to our desired site;*

*That her journey be safe,
sound, and swift,*

And divine providence be our gift.

*I petition the Goddess to
protect this space.*

May all who ride here be held in grace.

This is not just a seasonal spell. With practice, it can become second nature. Each time you get behind the wheel, pause and intone the first two lines.

Dallas Jennifer Cobb

May 9
Sunday

4th ♈

☽ v/c 6:50 pm

☽ → ♉ 7:46 pm

Color of the Day: Gold
Incense of the Day: Marigold

Mother's Day

The Great Mother

Today is Mother's Day, a holiday of nurturing, love, and appreciation. It has been celebrated in many ways across time and cultures. Most involve giving flowers or other gifts to your mother, while others have focused on reconciliation and world peace. A more practical approach is to throw parties to teach parenting skills.

As Pagans, we revere the Goddess in her guise as the Great Mother. Her generosity and fecundity make life possible. Take some time today for a ritual in her honor. Decorate your altar with a floral cloth or spring flowers. Thank the Goddess for the abundance and blessings in your life. Speak to her about your relationship with your mother, and if you are a mother yourself, talk about your relationship(s) with your child(ren) too. Do something to make your home a nurturing place. If you like, add a pledge to do something for mothers in your community. For cakes and ale, enjoy milk and cookies!

Elizabeth Barrette

May 10
Monday

4th ♉

Color of the Day: Silver
Incense of the Day: Rosemary

World Bird Migration Day

Birds play an important part in secular and earth-based belief systems. Appreciate the joy in listening to their songs and calls and watching them at domestic feeders and in their natural habitats.

Does your personal or family totem honor a special bird? Take some time today to trace their migratory habits. Or, if you have no special feathered friend, perhaps take some time to research the birds in your area and see which one calls to your spirit of flight.

Obtain a bird book for your area, close your eyes, flip the pages, and stop! Is this your spirit bird?

Emyme

May 11
Tuesday

4th ♉

New Moon 3:00 pm

Color of the Day: White
Incense of the Day: Cedar

Ramadan ends

A May New Moon Spell

A May new moon is a perfect time to energize your spirit. This spell will empower your spirit, and at the same time help you achieve a wish. Think of a wish as you prepare for this ritual. First, cover your altar with dark blue fabric. Upon the altar place one dark blue candle and a vase of spring flowers. Lilacs, pansies, and violets are good. Safely light the candle. Think of your wish as you chant the following verse three times:

As the May moon begins to grow,

So does the magical seed I sow!

These flowers live, these flowers wither,

But my spirit shall live forever.

Meditate upon your wish, then snuff out the candle. You may use the candle again for magic. Leave the flowers on your altar until they fade. When the flowers wither, place them gently on the ground outside. As the flowers return to Mother Earth, your wish will grow to fruition.

James Kambos

May 12
Wednesday

1st ♉

☽ v/c 8:23 am

☽ → ♊ 8:43 am

Color of the Day: Brown
Incense of the Day: Lavender

Think of Me Tulip Spell

Tulips are associated with love and new beginnings. Send a message to your sweetheart with this easy spell.

You will need some lipstick, gloss, or balm and a petal from a red tulip. Close your eyes and think of a message you'd like to send to someone you adore. Put the lipstick or balm on your lips and say "think of me" three times while visualizing their face. Kiss the tulip petal, leaving a clear imprint.

Go to a place where traffic, the wind, or a body of water is flowing in your sweetheart's direction, and discreetly let the tulip petal slip from your fingers. (Do not do this in the traffic. On the sidewalk will do.) They will be reminded of you sometime that day as the energy of the tulip petal gets carried toward them.

Kate Freuler

May 13
Thursday

1st ♊

Color of the Day: Green
Incense of the Day: Myrrh

Nature Fairy Spell

The fairies are always around to assist you. It is a good idea to show them gratitude for their help along your spiritual journey.

Walk into the woods or an outdoor area with lots of trees. Gather up nuts, seeds, leaves, and stones that you find on your path. Find a flat surface on a rock or an area in the grass at the base of a tree, and arrange the items in a circular pattern to create a nature mandala as an offering. Close your eyes, take a deep breath, and chant this three times:

I am grateful for this day.

I am grateful for the fae.

I've created this beautiful nature art.

*Please accept it as a gift
from my grateful heart.*

Know that the fairies appreciate your heartfelt nature offering and will continue to guide and assist you on your magical path.

Sapphire Moonbeam

May 14
Friday

1st ♊

☽ v/c 6:51 am

☽ → ♋ 9:30 pm

Color of the Day: Pink
Incense of the Day: Cypress

Contentment Spell

To increase peace and satisfaction in your life, light a pink candle and anoint the candle with rose, gardenia, or sweetpea essential oil. These scents promote harmony, peace, and happiness. Take a deep breath, and as you inhale the floral aroma, exhale with a sigh and visualize any self-doubt and negativity that's holding you back being expelled. Breathe in again and see yourself breathing in only feelings of joy and peace. Chant:

I am content, at peace, and calm.

My breath becomes a healing balm.

When I feel ill at ease,

All I have to do is breathe.

Allow the candle to burn out safely. Recall this moment anytime you need to feel content and take several deep breaths, repeating the chant.

Ember Grant

May 15
Saturday

1st ♋

Color of the Day: Gray
Incense of the Day: Sage

Grow Something

As Witches and Pagans, we do our best to connect with the earth and the natural world. One of the easiest ways to do that is to grow something. It doesn't really matter what, and there are plenty of choices no matter where you live or whether or not you have a green thumb. If you have a yard, by all means plant a flower, a vegetable garden, a bush, or a tree. But even if you only have a windowsill, you can grow an herb or two, or some beautiful flowers. If you want something to grow with your kids, you can even do something fun like grow a potato from a potato. The idea is simply to plant something in the soil, tend it, and watch it grow.

If you want to add an extra magical element, write down something you wish to have grow in your life and tuck the piece of paper into the soil. Then send your energy into that wish whenever you tend the plant.

Deborah Blake

May 16
Sunday

1st ♋

Color of the Day: Orange
Incense of the Day: Almond

Shavuot begins at sundown

Spirit Guide Clarity Spell

Happy Sunday! Jupiter recently entered the sign of Pisces, and we are looking at the beginning of a yearlong cycle of spiritual rebirth. Today is the perfect day to ruminate on your path and to audit your relationships to the people, places, and things that are connected to it. What we all could use now more than ever is a clear connection with our spirit allies as they help shape the road ahead.

Take a few moments tonight to ground and center your energy, then light a white candle in the east. After you light this candle, take a few breaths and focus on your spirit allies, then focus on the possibility of there being more allies that you don't know about. Say:

Spirit allies on the edge of vision,

Be with me through each decision.

Make yourself known so I can see.

Be here now and reveal yourself to me.

Let the candle burn out safely on its own.

Devin Hunter

May 17
Monday

1st ♋

☽ v/c 2:23 am

☽ → ♌ 8:44 am

Color of the Day: Lavender
Incense of the Day: Lily

Magical Infused Sugar

At this time of year, spring is in full force and the sun is in Taurus, which is an earth sign that rules over material pleasures, stability, and sensuality. To further your enjoyment of the season and add some magic to your meals, try making infused sugar! You can infuse practically any kind of sugar with your favorite herbs, spices, and floral elements (even coffee!), and then add them to your baking, your favorite beverages, or your magical workings.

To infuse sugar, mix four parts sugar to one part flavoring, the drier the better to avoid clumping. Stronger-smelling herbs may require a bit less. Store your mixture in a clean, airtight jar. Try rose petals for love, cinnamon for success, orange for creativity, or coffee beans for energy. The possibilities are infinite. Allow the flavors to infuse for two to three weeks before using the sugar.

Thorn Mooney

May 18
Tuesday

1st ♌

Color of the Day: Maroon
Incense of the Day: Geranium

Fiery Protection

Tuesday brings us the fiery energy of Mars. Red jasper, one of my favorite stones, is also associated with Mars. Today is a great day to harness red jasper's qualities for some well-needed protection magic.

One of my favorite things about red jasper is that it brings wonderful healing energies along with its protective energy, making it a favorite of healers and energy workers. Find a small tumbled red jasper to which you feel drawn. Sit comfortably, hold the stone up to your heart, and close your eyes. Feel the stone's energy vibrating. Visualize its energy as a fiery but comforting deep red light emanating from the stone and surrounding your energy body. When you are enveloped in the comforting glow, slowly open your eyes and become aware of your surroundings. Carry the stone on your person in a pocket or pouch. May you glean healing and protection!

Blake Octavian Blair

May 19
Wednesday

1st ♌

☽ v/c 3:13 pm
2nd Quarter 3:13 pm
☽ → ♍ 4:59 pm

Color of the Day: Yellow
Incense of the Day: Bay laurel

Lights, Camera, Magick!

It seems we can't turn on our TV, computer, or smartphone without seeing the latest ad for a film or TV show that highlights Witchcraft. Let's face it: Witchcraft is hot these days, and everyone wants to get in on traditions or a way of life that once upon a time would have only been talked about behind closed doors or in hushed circles.

For this spell we're going to celebrate the lasting power of the Craft and its ability to come out of the broom closet. You will need a broom and some salted water.

Sprinkle the salted water on your broom. Hold the broom high above your head. Turn three times clockwise and say:

Once we were in the dark. What was once in the shadows lives in the light. To the Witches, may our power continue to take flight!

Najah Lightfoot

May 20
Thursday

2nd ♏

☉ → ♊ 3:37 pm

Color of the Day: White
Incense of the Day: Mulberry

Invoking the Spirit

For this spell you will need a small mirror and five candles with holders in the following colors: yellow, red, blue, green, and violet.

Arrange the yellow, red, blue, and green candles on the floor in a large circle, representing the four physical elemental powers. Sit on the floor in the middle of them, with the mirror and violet candle in front of you.

Ground and center. Light each of the first four candles in turn while contemplating the elemental presence they represent. You might imagine streams of elementally colored light flowing from the cardinal directions and into the unlit central violet candle.

Now light the violet candle and say:

Four sacred things in this place be

Combined to call the fifth to me,

By four made one I call you forth,

By spirit's song I call you in.

Begin to chant a low drone (such as "Om") until you feel a light buzzing in your body. Gaze into the mirror and allow yourself to scry, watching for subtle images to appear in the mirror or in your mind's eye. Feel the presence of spirit!

Storm Faerywolf

Notes:

May 21
Friday

2nd ♏

☽ v/c 3:56 pm

☽ → ♎ 9:35 pm

Color of the Day: Coral

Incense of the Day: Violet

Getting Your Point Across

The sun recently entered Gemini, the sign of communication. That power can be harnessed to create understanding where there is confusion. If someone has been unable to grasp a point you've been trying to make, write a letter to them explaining exactly what you mean, then copy it down on another piece of paper. One paper you will keep, and the other you will use in this spell.

With the flame of an orange candle, carefully light an incense charcoal in a cauldron and burn some dried marjoram. Now read your letter, imagining that you're speaking directly to the intended recipient. After you've read it, light the paper in the candle's flame, dropping it in the cauldron on top of the incense, and say:

Gemini power, your aid I seek, with smoke and flame of Mercury; my message delivered to whom I speak, understood at last, so mote it be.

Be sure to extinguish the candle.

Michael Furie

May 22
Saturday

2nd ♎

Color of the Day: Black
Incense of the Day: Rue

A May Love Spell

In May, all growing things are pulsing with the life force. This love spell taps into that power. You'll need the following items:

- 2 red taper candles in holders
- A few drops of almond oil
- A pinch each of basil, cinnamon, and clove
- A small square piece of red fabric
- Red ribbon

First, rub the oil onto each candle, then set each candle in a holder. Combine the herbs in the center of the fabric, and tie the corners together with ribbon. Safely light the candles. Hold the herb bundle and say:

The seed sprouts, the bud swells.
Earth power, hear this spell.

I light candles of ruby red.
Send me the one who'll turn my head.

I combine love herbs three.
Let them send a perfect love to me.

Love, find me by this candlelight.
Guard me as I speak these
words tonight.

Lastly, snuff out the candles. When romance finds you, dispose of the candles and the herb bundle.

James Kambos

NOTES:

May 23
Sunday

2nd ♎

☽ v/c 5:36 pm

☽ → ♏ 11:00 pm

Color of the Day: Gold
Incense of the Day: Juniper

Bless and Multiply My Money

What we focus on grows, so create a prosperity altar to bless and multiply your money.

Gather coins and bills, flowers, herbs, stones, fossils, and other energized, magical objects. On a flat surface, create a spiral with about an eight-inch circumference. Lay the coins, bills, and other sacred objects down in ever smaller revolutions of the spiral. As you do this, think about how much money has been given to you throughout your life. Say:

Lucky me.

As you place the objects in smaller revolutions of the spiral, recognize how much money you currently have. Say:

Blessed me.

Recognize how, through employment and self-employment, you have money flowing regularly. Say:

Wealthy me.

As the spiral grows tighter and more condensed, incant:

Bless and multiply my money.

Make a small cluster of money at the center of the spiral and say:

Money flows to me easily and fluidly.

Over time, add found money and money-shaped candy to your altar. This will keep your attention focused on the growth of your money. Each time, say:

Bless and multiply my money.
                                    Dallas Jennifer Cobb

NOTES:

May 24
Monday

2nd ♏

Color of the Day: Gray
Incense of the Day: Hyssop

Victoria Day (Canada)

New Life for hand-Me-Downs

Physical objects retain the energy of those who created or used them. When bringing any piece of furniture into your home, it is always wise to cleanse it. Family furniture passed down through the generations may be infused with considerable and varied forces. When bringing in items from relatives we know and love, the cleansing may be less stringent. A simple request and a "blessed be" might suffice, or only a light saging may be needed. One way to be sure the positive essence remains and impart your own energy is by refinishing or refurbishing the piece. Many items will most certainly benefit from a sprucing up. When you are done, offer up this heartfelt spell:

This (name of item) has served
the family well. I'll give this
piece a newer face and keep it
with care in a special place.

Emyme

May 25
Tuesday

2nd ♏
☽ v/c 5:20 pm
☽ → ♐ 10:39 pm

Color of the Day: Scarlet
Incense of the Day: Bayberry

Lucky Coin Spell

For this spell you will need a shiny coin and three drops of sunflower oil.

Take the coin and oil to a sunny place outdoors if possible. Hold the coin in such a way that it reflects the light of the sun. Imagine the sun filling it up with warmth, joy, and positivity. Place the oil onto the coin and rub it in with your fingers. As you do so, imagine a bright yellow sunflower, its open face basking in the sun. The coin is now imbued with bright positive vibrations. Carry it with you and pay attention to what happens throughout your day. Take notice of any seemingly lucky or especially nice or pleasant situations you experience—including the small things.

The following day, place the coin on a sidewalk or path where you know someone will find it and pick it up, passing on the good luck to whoever carries it.

Kate Freuler

May 26
Wednesday

2nd ♐

Full Moon 7:14 am

Color of the Day: Brown
Incense of the Day: Honeysuckle

Lunar Eclipse

Flower Moon Bath

The full moon in May is known as the Flower Moon. In the spirit of the season of flowers, it is a perfect time to have a full moon bath. Water not only cleanses our spirit but also heals us.

Prepare a bath after the sun goes down by adding petals from your favorite flowers. You can also add drops of essential oils to uplift and enhance the energies you want to grow and bloom in your life. Add drops of lavender or lemon oil for peace, rose oil or ginger for love, and vanilla, parsley, or thyme oil for happiness and joy.

As you soak in the fragrant water, focus on your dreams and desires and envision them manifesting in your life. Remove the petals before draining the water, but let the water completely drain as you remain in the tub. This bath can be done again up to two days after the full moon to increase the effectiveness of the spell.

Sapphire Moonbeam

May 27
Thursday

3rd ♐

☽ v/c 1:35 pm

☽ → ♑ 10:23 pm

Color of the Day: Crimson
Incense of the Day: Apricot

Cell Phone Protection

Most cell phones are fragile. A brisk bump, a short fall, or more than a few drops of rain can ruin one. Yet people take their cell phones everywhere, in all kinds of conditions, which leads to accidents and broken devices.

For this protection spell, you will need a cell phone case printed with a spider and/or a spiderweb. Think of Grandmother Spider, whose sphere of influence includes all webs and networks, along with communication from afar. Hold the spiderweb case between your hands and say:

Grandmother Spider, spin your web,

Subtle and silken, line by line.

Spin your magic across this case,

Keeping this cell phone working fine.

Put the case on the phone. Visualize the web protecting the cell phone from all harm, and trace over the web with your finger. Say the spell again. The cell phone is now protected. If you ever need a boost of protection, repeat the spell.

Elizabeth Barrette

May 28
Friday

3rd ♑

Color of the Day: Purple
Incense of the Day: Rose

De-stress Meditation

Many people use lavender to alleviate headaches or to create a calming atmosphere. Inhale the aroma of lavender, either by using essential oil in a diffuser, applying it diluted to the skin, or crushing some dried lavender between your fingers. As you breathe in the scent, visualize yourself being calm and centered.

Chant this three times:

Lavender, lavender, bring me peace.

Lavender, lavender, stress decrease.

Ember Grant

May 29
Saturday

3rd ♑

☽ v/c 6:15 pm

Color of the Day: Blue
Incense of the Day: Pine

Contentment Stone

It can be hard enough to accept life on a good day, but it's on the really difficult days that we need hope and luck the most. Cast the following spell on a found stone, anointing it with lavender oil and speaking to it this incantation:

A rolling stone gathers no moss, about the world it is effortlessly tossed.

But this little gem took an adventure again, standing before my toes, as lost as Faust.

From the greatest mountain to the smallest stone, I am content with all that I have known.

Keep the stone in your wallet to remind you to be grateful for every little thing you have. Use the luck that is all around you. Learn to see it and appreciate it by recognizing the value and sentient consciousness in everything that exists.

Estha McNevin

May 30
Sunday

3rd ♑

☽ → ♒ 12:04 am

Color of the Day: Amber
Incense of the Day: Eucalyptus

Spell to Reveal a Mystery

The purpose of this spell is to inspire a dream to reveal a mystery that has been locked away from you. You will need these materials:

- A purple candle
- Some ground cinnamon
- A pen or pencil
- A piece of unlined paper
- A piece of chalk
- A key to an unknown lock

In the dark of night, gather your items and focus on your mystery. Sprinkle the candle with some cinnamon and light it with a silent prayer. With the pen or pencil, write your mystery on the paper, then use chalk to draw a large circle around it. Place the key in the center of the circle, saying:

A mystery in a circle of chalk,

A key that goes to no known lock.

What has been locked away, concealed,

My dreams now open and reveal.

Allow the candle to burn down safely, then sleep with the key under your pillow. The next morning, bury the key on your property. Watch your dreams for an answer to your prayer!

Storm Faerywolf

NOTES:

May 31
Monday

3rd ≈≈

Color of the Day: White
Incense of the Day: Clary sage

Memorial Day

A Light for Those We've Lost

It's Memorial Day here in the US, and that means it's time to remember those we have lost as a result of active military service. No matter where you live, chances are someone you know has experienced loss due to war or combat, so here is a little spell to guide the lost back home.

Light a red candle in the north and recite these words:

Lost to the living but not from our hearts, I light this flame to guide all your parts.

Have peace in mind and no longer worry; peace in soul, rest, there's no hurry.

Your war is over, no battles to win, by this candle the veil is thin.

Come home, soldier, if you've been lost, you've fought all you can and paid the cost.

Allow the candle to safely burn out on its own.

Devin Hunter

June

The month of June is a time that inspires warmth, love, passion, and deep appreciation of beauty. Agricultural festivals in old Europe acknowledge and celebrate the many flowers and fruits that become abundant at this time. It is no coincidence that these plants—such as roses, raspberries, strawberries, wildflowers, and those that feature red or pink flowers or fruit—are associated with the planet Venus and the goddess Aphrodite. June is also the traditional month for weddings, and the term *honeymoon* refers to the beverage mead, made from fermented honey, that was traditionally given to the bride and groom as an aphrodisiac.

June brings the start of summer, and for thousands of years the summer solstice has been a prominent festival in many cultures. This celestial festival signifies the beginning of warm weather and abundant growth yet also reminds us of its opposite calendar festival: the winter solstice. All hail the Holly King! Spells done in June are often connected to love, romance, growth, health, and abundance.

Peg Aloi

June 1
Tuesday

3rd ≈≈

☽ v/c 2:14 am

☽ → ♓ 5:07 am

Color of the Day: Black
Incense of the Day: Ginger

Out with the Bad, In with the Good

To cleanse yourself and your home of any bad vibes and then charge up the area with beneficial energy, burn an incense composed of equal parts frankincense and myrrh, with a pinch of dried orange peel for added energy. With an incense charcoal and a heatproof censer, and moving in a clockwise motion, travel from room to room in your home with the incense, using the smoke to cleanse the space while repeating the following:

Spirits purified, auras cleansed,
from this moment the misfortune ends.

Any harm sent this way shall
lose its power by light of day.

Once you have treated each room, extinguish the incense and take a shower to rid yourself of any residual bad vibes.

Michael Furie

June 2
Wednesday

3rd ♓

4th Quarter 3:24 am

Color of the Day: Topaz
Incense of the Day: Lavender

Open Communication

To clear the way for open communication in any setting, try this spell. Light a yellow candle and, if you have one, place a double-terminated clear quartz point in front of the candle. Visualize the parties involved being open with each other and information flowing freely and easily between everyone. Imagine the crystal conducting the communication back and forth through each point. Chant:

Clear the way, let all be heard.

Open the way for every word.

Allow the candle to burn out safely. Carry the crystal with you anytime you're with the people in the group for which the spell is intended.

Ember Grant

June 3
Thursday

4th ♓

☽ v/c 7:10 am

☽ → ♈ 1:59 pm

Color of the Day: Green
Incense of the Day: Clove

Anointing Oil for Tools

It's that time of year when our garden tools get dusted off and put back to work. This repair oil is a good way to keep wooden handles smooth and able to endure the harsh and muddy conditions of the garden. Combine the following oils in a glass bottle with a fitted screw cap:

- 1 cup liquid coconut oil
- 8 drops frankincense essential oil
- 2 drops orange essential oil
- 3 drops holy basil essential oil
- 3 drops ylang-ylang essential oil
- 3 tablespoons liquid calendula essential oil
- 3 tablespoons jojoba essential oil

Begin by cleaning the tools very well with a solution of soapy water and vinegar. Dry them thoroughly to avoid any cracks or warped results later. Begin massaging the repair oil from the base to the tip, and do your best to think fertile and virile thoughts, as well as focused prayers to our Mother Earth. When done, store the tools for the next use and enjoy another season of splinter-free gardening.

Estha McNevin

NOTES:

June 4
Friday

4℔ ♈︎

Color of the Day: Pink
Incense of the Day: Yarrow

A Diverse Magical Community

Throughout Canada, Australia, and the United States, June is celebrated as Pride Month, honoring members of the LBGTQ2 communities and recognizing the Stonewall rebellion of 1969, which resulted in recognition of gay rights under the law in the US.

Today, do a small diversity spell, drawing in the spirit element, building pride and acceptance in your community, and affirming your diverse magical community.

Gather seven small items, each of a different color, thinking of seven people in your community of different ages, genders, ethnicities, cultures, orientations, and occupations.

Place these totems on your altar, circled around a candle of any color. As you safely light the candle, whisper:

Every one of you is welcome,
different, unique, and bright.

Every one of you is perfect,
different, unique, and right.

Come together in diversity.

Come together including me.

Come together that we can be

A diverse magical community.

So mote it be.

Be sure to extinguish the candle.

Dallas Jennifer Cobb

NOTES:

June 5
Saturday

4th ♈

☽ v/c 6:47 pm

Color of the Day: Indigo
Incense of the Day: Ivy

healing the Earth

Today is World Environment Day. Work some magic to heal the earth. Druids considered oak to be a sacred tree, so plant an oak today. In the eastern United States, choose red or white oak. In the mountains, scrub oak grows. In the South and on the West Coast, pick live oak. In the North, bur oak thrives. For marshy areas, try swamp white oak. For dry, sandy soil, try scarlet oak.

Plant your oak in a sunny, open area. Dig a big hole and put in the sapling. Mix plenty of compost into the loose soil, then pack it around the roots. Top with a layer of mulch, preferably composted oak leaves. Then say:

Tree of life, I give life to you so that you may give life to the forest.

Water the sapling thoroughly. Then say:

Water of life, may you give life to the oak.

Elizabeth Barrette

June 6
Sunday

4th ♈

☽ → ♉ 1:46 am

Color of the Day: Orange
Incense of the Day: Hyacinth

Egg Spell for Release

For this spell you will need an egg and a permanent marker. Sit outside or in a window under the waning moon while holding the egg in your palm. Think about the things in your life that are holding you back from achieving your potential. This could be attachments to toxic people, bad habits, negative self-talk, or any other things that you'd like to be free of. As you contemplate these problems, write them down on the egg in small letters, covering the entire shell if you wish. Go into as much detail as you like, feeling the unwanted circumstances transfer from you into the egg. Visualize the yolk inside the egg as containing all the energy of the problems.

Go outdoors and dig a small hole in the ground. Crack the egg and bury the yolk in the hole. Walk away, knowing you've left your problems behind. Compost or dispose of the shells.

Kate Freuler

June 7
Monday

4ħ ☿

Color of the Day: Ivory
Incense of the Day: Neroli

A Grass Love Spell

Use this spell before a wedding or a handfasting, or just to strengthen any romance. It should be performed with your romantic partner. You'll need a small grapevine wreath. To perform this spell, go to a field where tall wild grasses are growing. Cut some grasses. With your partner, twist the grass around the wreath until it's covered with grass. As you do so, together say:

*Like this circle, our love is
unbroken and round.*

*These grasses we secure
around and around*

Are like our love, forever bound.

*Our love shall deepen as these
grasses return to the ground.*

End by laying the wreath on the ground among some growing grass. Let the wreath and grass decay and return to the womb of Mother Earth. As they do, your love will strengthen.

James Kambos

 June 8
Tuesday

4ħ ☿

☽ v/c 11:07 am

☽ → ♊ 2:47 pm

Color of the Day: Red
Incense of the Day: Basil

Storm's Oatmeal Abundance Cookies

Oatmeal cookies have many ingredients associated with money and abundance. As you perform this spell, contemplate each ingredient and feel how they are all part of the magic. You will need:

- 1 cup (2 sticks) butter, softened
- 1 ¼ cups brown sugar, firmly packed
- ½ cup granulated sugar
- 2 eggs
- 2 teaspoons vanilla
- 1 ½ cups all-purpose flour
- 1 teaspoon baking soda
- ½ teaspoon salt
- 2 teaspoons cinnamon
- 3 cups uncooked oatmeal
- 1 ¼ cups raisins
- 2 tablespoons unsweetened applesauce
- ⅛ teaspoon ground cloves
- Pinch of nutmeg

Preheat oven to 350°F. In a mixing bowl, beat together butter and sugars until creamy. Add eggs and vanilla, and beat until smooth.

In a separate bowl, combine flour, baking soda, and salt. Sprinkle cinnamon on top in the shape of a dollar sign. Mix together. Add to the dough.

Add the oats, raisins, applesauce, cloves, and nutmeg. Mix well.

Drop by rounded tablespoonfuls onto an ungreased cookie sheet.

Bake 10–12 minutes or until golden brown.

Cool 1 minute on the cookie sheet before removing to a wire rack.

Offer a cookie to the spirits of the land. The rest are to be enjoyed.

Storm Faerywolf

June 9
Wednesday

4th ♊

Color of the Day: White
Incense of the Day: Marjoram

Honoring Vesta

Historically there was only one time every year when Vesta's temple was open to the public: during the festival of Vestalia, held from June 7–15. Even then, only females were permitted to enter, and they had to petition for blessings on behalf of the rest of their family and household. Thankfully, these days most of the progressive pagan community has moved beyond such gender segregation, so let's all take the opportunity today to honor this goddess of hearth and home.

For many of us, our home is our temple. Today, make an offering to Vesta of some home-cooked food from your kitchen hearth. It doesn't matter if it's elaborate or simple— perhaps a lovely bit of homemade bread or even a cup of tea made yourself. Place it on your altar and safely light a candle to Vesta. Ask for a blessing upon your hearth, home, and family. Be sure to extinguish the candle. Blessed be!

Blake Octavian Blair

June 10
Thursday

4th ♊

New Moon 6:53 am

☽ v/c 1:38 pm

Color of the Day: Turquoise
Incense of the Day: Carnation

Solar Eclipse

Eclipse Spell to Find the Lost

The world is buzzing today, with the solar eclipse in the air. Did you know eclipses are particularly good to work with for finding lost objects? They help reveal the things that remain hidden, especially when those things are in plain sight!

To cast this spell, you'll need one small white candle and one small black candle. The bigger the candle, the longer it will take for the spell to work. Anoint the candles with a small amount of eucalyptus essential oil (or camphor oil). Hold the black candle and say:

You! You are (the thing that is missing) and I am going to find you!

Then light the black candle. When the candle has burned down about halfway, hold the white candle in your hand and say:

What was hidden is now revealed!

Then light the white candle from the black candle. Allow both to burn out safely on their own. Keep an eye out for synchronicities and have an open mind. Usually the lost object reveals itself within forty-eight hours.

Devin Hunter

NOTES:

June 11
Friday

1st ♊

☽ → ♋ 3:23 am

Color of the Day: Rose
Incense of the Day: Alder

Take Back the Night

With the days growing longer as we approach the summer solstice, June is a delightful time to perform some night magic, even if you aren't a huge fan of the dark. As I age, my night vision grows worse, and often the darkness leaves me feeling more vulnerable to falling. It's been a long, dark winter.

Tonight, take back the night by going for an evening walk. Sunset will occur today at 8:52 p.m. here in the Eastern time zone on the north side of Lake Ontario. Only a few short months ago, it would have been completely dark hours earlier.

Depart on your walk in time to be outdoors and facing west as the sun is setting. Pause, give thanks for the long days of light, and take back the night hours as yours to enjoy for the next few weeks. Then turn around and walk back home in the growing dusk.

Dallas Jennifer Cobb

June 12
Saturday

1st ♋

Color of the Day: Black
Incense of the Day: Sage

Blessings, Gifts, and Opportunities

Each morning brings an opportunity to gives thanks and gratitude for a new day and new beginning. Each night brings an opportunity to give thanks and reflect upon our day before we close our eyes for sleep. Whether the day has been good or bad, we can always find one thing for which to be grateful.

We are powerful beings. We have the ability to call forth and manifest. Today, give thanks for all the blessings, gifts, and opportunities you have received. Use your power to keep calling goodness into your life by sincerely connecting with your higher power or deity. Say:

Thank you for all the blessings, gifts, and opportunities I have received.

And thank you for all the blessings, gifts, and opportunities that are on their way to me right now.

Use this mantra on a daily basis to keep the energy and power of good juju flowing in your life.

Najah Lightfoot

June 13
Sunday

1st ♋

☽ v/c 7:16 am

☽ → ♌ 2:22 pm

Color of the Day: Gold
Incense of the Day: Juniper

Candle Tips

Before lighting a new candle for a spell, check to make sure that you have peeled off all the wrappers and labels. Some candles have a layer of clear plastic shrink-wrapped around them that is hard to see and will smoke if the candle is lit.

You can dedicate any candle for a certain spell or ritual by using a pin to carve a name, runes, or other magical symbols down the side. If you don't like handling sharp things, a dried-out ballpoint pen also works well.

If a candle builds up a pool of melted wax that threatens to drown the flame, you can tilt the candle or press a metal tool against the rim of wax to make a channel so that some of the wax can run out.

When a candle wick burns down too low to light but there is still plenty of wax in the rest of the candle, carve a well around the wick in order to make it long enough to burn.

Elizabeth Barrette

June 14
Monday

1st ♌

Color of the Day: Lavender
Incense of the Day: Lily

Flag Day

Magic Circles Day

June 14 is Magic Circles Day. A circle is used in ritual ceremonies to focus and raise the energy inside the perimeter. Creating the circle, or magical barrier, can be done in a number of ways. You can use an athame, also known as a ritual knife, to draw the circle energetically. If you don't have ritual tools, you can simply use your pointer finger and envision the circle as a color of light. Your body and mind are the only things you really need to create powerful magick. You can use salt to create a physical barrier for protection while in the circle. Stones and crystals or candles can be used, with fire safety in mind. When the circle is cast, say:

> Let nothing but love enter and
> let nothing but love leave.

Perform the spell of your choice. Then take down the circle, visualizing it dissolving in the opposite direction of how it was created.

Sapphire Moonbeam

June 15
Tuesday

1st ♏ ♌

☽ v/c 1:27 pm

☽ → ♏ 11:02 pm

Color of the Day: Gray
Incense of the Day: Geranium

Smooth Travels

As the school year comes to a close and summer is upon us, many people embark on vacations. Traveling can be a wonderful experience, whether you go by yourself or with others, looking for adventure or for relaxation. Here's a simple spell to help things go smoothly, no matter what kind of trips you take.

Place a symbol of your journey (this can be anything from a picture of where you're going to a toy car or plane) in front of a white candle in a firesafe candleholder or dish. Put a large square of aluminum foil under the candleholder, making sure the piece is large enough to put at least partially around your symbol. Then say the following while gently pulling up the foil so it surrounds the candle and your symbol like a low wall. (Snuff out the candle when done.)

Protection like a bubble,

To keep the journey smooth.

Safe travels without trouble,

All obstacles remove.

Deborah Blake

 June 16
Wednesday

1st ♏

Color of the Day: Yellow
Incense of the Day: Honeysuckle

Spell for a New Houseplant

Even if you're not much of a gardener, summer is a great time to bring plants into your life to add both beauty and magic. Consider adding a houseplant or two to brighten your home. Choose cacti for protection, African violet for love and working with fairies, aloe for health and healing, or pothos for longevity and success. Speak to your plants and consciously charge them with a task in the household. When you bring a new plant home, concentrate on its purpose and say:

Welcome home, friend. I ask that
you bring your own magic to this
home. I will care for you, and
together let us be partners.

Write your specific instructions for your new plant on a slip of rice paper and bury it in the soil to decompose. As the plant grows and flourishes, its magic will come to fruition. Be sure to research and provide any special care your plant may require so you can return the favor!

Thorn Mooney

June 17
Thursday

1st ♍

☽ v/c 11:54 pm

2nd Quarter 11:54 pm

Color of the Day: Purple
Incense of the Day: Mulberry

Safe Travel Spell for Yourself or Loved Ones

Whether you find traveling to be a joy or a chore, we all have to do it from time to time. For those occasions when there may be safety concerns, a bit of magical defense is handy to use.

Envision the person (or people) to be protected surrounded by a silvery bubble of protection. Make this mental image as strong as possible, and infuse into it all the love and concern you have for the person. When you feel that the power is at its peak, say:

By hoof, by wheel, by boat or plane,

Be safe in all travel and return again;

Healthy and whole, protected yet free,

As I do will, so shall it be.

This spell can be repeated as often as desired.

Michael Furie

 June 18
Friday

2nd ♍

☽ → ♎ 4:54 am

Color of the Day: White
Incense of the Day: Vanilla

Strengthen Bonds

To reinforce the bonds in a relationship of any kind, begin by writing your name and the other person's name on the same sheet of paper. This works best if both people participate, each writing their own name. Fold the paper as many times as you can and place it in a heatproof dish. Set a pink or white candle on top of the paper. As you light the candle, visualize the relationship between you growing stronger. After the candle has burned out safely, take what's left of it, and the paper, and bury them someplace safe. As you bury these items, hold hands and say these words together:

*Let our relationship stay
healthy and strong.*

*Keep trust between us, and if
something goes wrong,*

Let us resolve it as soon as we can.

Let this be true if we both understand.

Ember Grant

June 19
Saturday

2nd ♎

Color of the Day: Brown
Incense of the Day: Magnolia

Coin Spell

Everyone could use a little prosperity. In the past, people often wore coins as jewelry to attract wealth. This spell draws on that history.

To cast this spell, you will need some wearable coinage, a paper and pen, and a sprig of fresh basil. Necklaces, bracelets, earrings, and bellydance scarves often have coin-like dangles. Some belt buckles have pennies or other coins welded onto a background. You can also find actual sunken treasure or other historic coins made up into jewelry, usually pendants or earrings. Rings and tie tacks are less common but occasionally feature coins.

First count how many coins you have on your jewelry. For each coin, write down an aspect of prosperity, such as attracting wealth or saving money. Now rub the basil over the first coin while chanting its aspect of prosperity. Imagine that aspect manifesting and what improvements it would make for you. Do the same with the remaining coins. Finally, bury the basil in your yard. Wear the jewelry when you need prosperity. You can keep the paper on your altar.

Elizabeth Barrette

NOTES:

June 20
Sunday

2nd ♎

☽ v/c 6:52 am

☽ → ♏ 7:58 am

☉ → ♋ 11:32 pm

Color of the Day: Yellow

Incense of the Day: Frankincense

Father's Day –
Litha – Summer Solstice

A Summer Solstice Solar Blessing

This ritual celebrates the sun god and the summer solstice. It should be performed at noon, the solar hour. If possible, perform this ritual outside.

You'll need one orange pillar candle and a bowl of water containing a few drops of orange extract. Place the candle on a sturdy surface outside, such as a table or a flat rock. If inside, use an altar or a table. In front of the candle, place the bowl with the water/extract. Safely light the candle and raise it skyward. Then set it down and say:

We have called you Helios, Ra,
and many other names.

You are the King of Light
and the eternal flame.

Bless me with the bounty
of your kingdom.

Bless me with your power
and your wisdom.

Now sprinkle the water/extract mixture about as an offering. Let the candle burn a few minutes, then extinguish it. This ends the spell. You may use the candle again for prosperity magic.

James Kambos

NOTES:

June 21
Monday

2nd ♏

Color of the Day: White
Incense of the Day: Clary sage

Strike a Pose!

June 21 is International Yoga Day! Yoga is well known as a practice of the body, mind, and spirit. It balances these elements of ourselves and is simultaneously grounding and uplifting. While yoga's cultural origins deserve great respect, let us have gratitude that this practice from ancient India now has a global presence.

Today, find and learn a simple yoga pose that you are physically able to do easily. (There are poses for all levels of physical ability.) Perform this yoga pose and take a few moments to pay attention to your breath. Use your breath and posture to focus on balancing yourself within and without. Feel yourself as part of the greater world around you.

Blake Octavian Blair

NOTES:

 # June 22
Tuesday

2nd ♏

☽ v/c 2:43 am

☽ → ♐ 8:55 am

Color of the Day: Scarlet
Incense of the Day: Bayberry

A Queer Love Spell

It's LGBTQ+ Pride month, and as an outspoken member of that community, I would like to offer this Queer Love Spell. (Straight people can use this too! Just alter the symbolism to fit your desired relationship.)

Gather these materials:

• Your computer and printer

• Paper

• Tape or glue

• Colored markers

• A candle and holder (extra points for a rainbow candle, but any color will do)

Decide on an appropriate symbol to represent each person in the relationship. For example, men might choose the astrological symbol for Mars (♂), since it traditionally represents male, including one for each person. Women might choose Venus (♀), representing female. Trans and nonbinary individuals might combine these. Or you could choose more personal symbols such as favorite animals, comic book characters, pop-culture icons, etc.

Print these symbols and arrange them with tape or glue onto a piece of paper, forming a collage and leaving the center clear. Use markers to draw a rainbow heart in the center, a symbol for our diverse community. Place the candle in the holder within the heart. Light the candle and say:

Hidden light and hidden love,

Into my life here be now drawn.

Let the candle burn down safely.

Storm Faerywolf

June 23
Wednesday

2nd ♐

☽ v/c 10:09 pm

Color of the Day: Brown
Incense of the Day: Lilac

Ritual Chalk

If you're like me, symbols and sigils play a large role in your practice. This all-purpose homemade chalk can be imbued with energy to enhance your magickal workings, then used to draw symbols on your tools, walls, or floors, or outdoors during spells. It can also be tweaked according to intent by changing up the herbs. The herbs suggested here create a protective chalk.

Gather these materials:

- Silicone molds like those used for baking (any shape is fine) or an ice cube tray

- Wax paper

- A small mixing bowl

- 1 cup plaster of Paris

- ½ cup warm water

- 1 teaspoon powdered rosemary, frankincense, or mayapple (a nonpoisonous substitute for mandrake root)

Line the molds (or the tray) with wax paper.

In the bowl, mix together the plaster of Paris, warm water, and herbs. As you stir the mixture clockwise, visualize purple and white light being mixed in with it. These are the colors of spiritual energy and magickal power.

Pour the mixture into the molds and let sit for 24 hours. When they're dry, release them from the molds and get creative!

Kate Freuler

June 24
Thursday

2nd ♐

☽ → ♑ 9:05 am

Full Moon 2:40 pm

Color of the Day: Crimson
Incense of the Day: Myrrh

Marriage Mojo Oil

There are so many moments when life slows down just enough to let us be fat and happy for a day. Together with your partner or best friend, take a moment over a pot of tea to write down some of your best memories together. Write these on bay leaves using edible ink pens.

When you're done, place the leaves in a jar with a cork cap and fill with olive oil. As you perform this project together, dedicate the bottle of oil to shared meals, healing body rubs, and moments of shared nourishment. Choosing an antique or special olive oil bottle with symbols of the moon, Venus, or goddess imagery will help to add a sense of prophecy and energy to your mojo oil. Visualize growing togetherness as you anoint romantic candles and love charms with this oil.

Estha McNevin

June 25
Friday

3rd ♑

Color of the Day: Coral
Incense of the Day: Thyme

To Shield the Heart

Both the sun and Venus are now in Cancer, making this the perfect time for love and emotional healing magic. It's also a good time to do cleansing work related to emotions and current and past negative relationships, and to do shielding work related to our emotional body. Not only are many people feeling a bit raw at this time, but they are leaning on close friends and family for support. Cast this spell to shield your emotional body so you can remain strong at this time.

Hold a piece of black tourmaline, rose quartz, or rhodonite under running water and say:

I have enough to deal with on my own.

*I do not have time for
seeds I've not sown.*

Keep the drama away from me,

And keep my heart light and free.

Keep the stone with you at all times and renew once a week as needed.

Devin Hunter

June 26
Saturday

3rd ♑

☽ v/c 8:49 am

☽ → ♒ 10:09 am

Color of the Day: Blue
Incense of the Day: Sandalwood

Dirt Spell

Dirt is cooling to the spirit. You can slip and slide and make mud pies from it.

You can place it in a bowl and set it on your altar. You can gather some from a graveyard to use when you falter.

You can plant a flower in it, or bury things you love in it, so they'll always be with you when you gaze upon them from above.

For this spell, gather some dirt. You can take some from your plants, your back yard, or even a bag of potting soil. Place the dirt in a bowl. Say:

Mother Earth, you know best.

I honor you with this earth and have faith you'll do the rest.

I remain humble, in awe of you,

For blessed Mother Earth, you always know what to do.

Najah Lightfoot

June 27
Sunday

3rd ♒

☽ v/c 3:08 pm

Color of the Day: Amber
Incense of the Day: Almond

Return to Joy and Innocence

When life gets too serious and stressful, it's a good idea to reminisce about your youthful, carefree days. If you need help remembering your innocent, childlike spirit, white clover flowers can help you with that.

Go to a grassy field where white clover is in bloom. Find a place to sit near the flowers at the base of a tree. Close your eyes, take a deep cleansing breath, and inhale the scent of the lovely clover flowers.

Once you have become more grounded with the earth, collect clover flowers to make a crown. Place the clovers in a circle on a flat surface. Lay each clover flower near the end of the stem of the flower next to it. Tie the end of the stem underneath the clover flower to form a simple crown Place the crown on your head while saying these words:

Help me remember when I was young, when life was simple with laughter and fun.

Infuse my spirit with my innocent ways. Help me recapture the joy of those days.

Sapphire Moonbeam

 June 28
Monday

3rd ≈

☽ → ♓ 1:51 pm

Color of the Day: Gray
Incense of the Day: Narcissus

Make Friends with Moonstone

June is one of only two months that has three different birthstones associated with it. One of these is moonstone, which is a favorite gemstone of Witches. No matter which month you were born in, now is a good time to become better acquainted with this beautiful opalescent form of feldspar. Moonstone is most commonly seen in its white hue, from which is gets its association with the moon, although it can also come in a coral pink, blue, or even rainbow color. Because it is white and seems to glow, moonstone has long been linked both to the moon and to goddesses, especially lunar deities such as Diana, Isis, and Selene, among others.

Take a piece of moonstone and hold it in your hands. Close your eyes and feel its energy, then offer it up to the goddess to bless:

Goddess, bless this stone

Dedicated to the moon and to you

And to all positive magical work.

So mote it be.

Deborah Blake

June 29
Tuesday

3rd ♓

Color of the Day: Red
Incense of the Day: Ylang-ylang

Name Your Residence

It is the custom in many countries to name their homes and properties. Some names are amusing ("Upson Downs"), some are geographic ("Riverside Manor"), and some are charming ("Rose Cottage"). Information about the residents may be in a name, like "La Maison des Belles Femmes,"which means the house of beautiful women.

Whether you share the name of your residence with the world in the shape of a plaque or signpost or keep it private for the family only, it is a fun idea to brainstorm a name for the place where you lay your head at night. Also, benevolent home spirits, (fairies, pixies, brownies, etc.) love and appreciate a named home and will keep their mischievous counterparts at bay. Invoke them:

This house, this home, the place I where lay my head at night, be blessed with this name, (name of home), for all to see or in my private heart. May the humans and spirits dwelling within be happy and healthy and know they are cherished.

Emyme

June 30
Wednesday

3rd ♓

☽ v/c 1:40 pm

☽ → ♈ 9:21 pm

Color of the Day: Yellow

Incense of the Day: Lavender

Attuning to Fire

Now that we've passed the summer solstice, the days are gradually growing shorter. Although the heat and relaxed pace of the season may lull us into thinking that the days go on forever, from here on out we will lose a few minutes of daylight every day. In many Western magical systems, summer is associated with the element of fire. To make the most of these days while they are still long and warm, attune to the element of fire.

Sit before a lit candle, a campfire, or any other flame you can access comfortably. Gaze at it and relax, allowing yourself to feel its heat. Know that this elemental flame is part of you and say:

Powers of fire, lend me your gifts
of passion, spontaneity, and the
knowledge of my own True Will.
Be with me this day. So mote it be.

Safely extinguish the flame.

Thorn Mooney

NOTES:

July

In 46 BCE, when Julius Caesar decided to reform the Roman lunar calendar, the names of the months were numbers. He moved the first of the year back to January, and, being the egoist he was, he renamed the fifth month (the month of his birth) for himself: Iulius (Julius, today's July). He also gave it a thirty-first day. (Then he named the next month after his heir, Augustus.)

July (the month of my birth, too) is high summer. In many places, it's the hottest month of the year. It's the month in which everything blooms until the heat of the sun makes flowers—and people—wilt and nearly melt.

What do I remember from my childhood Julys? Rereading my favorite books. Dragging the big old washtub out on the side lawn, filling it with cold water, and splashing all afternoon. Helping my father tend his flowers—roses, columbines, tulips, and hydrangeas. Climbing to the very top of our neighbor's huge weeping willow tree. Chasing fireflies before bedtime and putting them in jars to glitter and wink throughout the night. Sleeping in the screened porch with all the windows open to catch every possible breeze. What are your favorite July memories?

Barbara Ardinger

July 1
Thursday

3rd ♈

4th Quarter 5:11 pm

Color of the Day: White
Incense of the Day: Balsam

Canada Day

Small but Mighty

Sometimes I'm mesmerized by the magnificence of a morning sunrise or the vibrant colors of an evening sunset. Then there are the exceptional moments when I'm transfixed, catapulted into worlds I didn't know existed, simply by gazing at a single drop of water lingering on the end of one of my plants.

Today may you find magick in the small, tiny, and undeniably spectacular things that cross your path. Take time to pick up something small or tiny, perhaps a rock, a stone, a button, or even a thimble, and gaze into the magnificent worlds only your inner eye and imagination can see.

Najah Lightfoot

 ## July 2
Friday

4th ♈

Color of the Day: Rose
Incense of the Day: Yarrow

A Spell to Spice Up Your Sex Life

Both Mars and Venus (who are famous in astrology for representing romantic/sexual relationships) are in Leo right now. The bad news is that you and your partner(s) might be more needy at this time. The good news is that you are bound to have some hot lovin' over the next few weeks. Be kind and direct and don't let things fester; face them instead and then get sensual about it. Cast this spell to add a little spice to the bedroom, literally.

Take two cinnamon sticks and tie them together in the shape of an X with red ribbon. Tie three knots on each leg with the ribbon. Chant the following until you have finished each knot:

Spice it up and let's get wild.

Turn it up to hot from mild!

Place the amulet under your bed and invite your partner(s) to have some adult time.

Devin Hunter

July 3
Saturday

4th ♈

☽ v/c 12:15 am
☽ → ♉ 8:28 am

Color of the Day: Black
Incense of the Day: Patchouli

Origami Divination

Try your luck today with this spell to boost memory and focus on spiritual issues. Choose a paper-folding design that is simple and fun, like the frog. On twelve pieces of paper, write random answers like "most likely," "perhaps not," and so on. Couple these with a quote from a spiritual text to employ humor, irony, and enlightenment all in one meme-worthy little note, such as "Never fry bacon in the nude," or something more serious like "Truth is mighty and shall prevail."

Then fold each piece of paper into the designated shape and spend the day distributing them to random people by chance or happenstance. Finding small ways to serve as a sounding board and inspiration for others will help any witch feel more closely connected to the thoughts and feelings of those around them. Random divination employs chaos and whimsy as well as our deep inner wisdom. Sharing your gifts will bring you a deep sense of joy and purpose.

Estha McNevin

NOTES:

July 4
Sunday

4th ☿

Color of the Day: Orange
Incense of the Day: Heliotrope

Independence Day

happy Independence Day

Today is Independence Day in the United States. Children are out of school, many people are on vacation, and baseball season is in full swing.

For this spell you will need:

- 3 chime (four-inch) candles: red, white, and blue
- Some Florida Water, which is readily available in botanicas and spiritual supply stores
- Olive oil
- 3 fireproof candleholders

Cleanse your candles with Florida Water, then anoint them with olive oil. Place them in their holders.

Light the red candle for veterans who suffer from PTSD and for whom fireworks can be extremely triggering.

Light the white candle for any independence you have achieved from things that no longer serve you.

Light the blue candle for fur babies, especially dogs who get scared of the sound of fireworks.

Allow your candles to safely burn down, or you can snuff them out and repeat this spell next year.

Najah Lightfoot

NOTES:

July 5
Monday

4th ♉

☽ v/c 12:57 pm

☽ → ♊ 9:24 pm

Color of the Day: Silver
Incense of the Day: Rosemary

The Calm after the Storm

In the United States, the Fourth of July is a holiday celebrated with parties and loud fireworks. For many, the fifth of July comes as something of a relief after all that noise and commotion. For most of us, holidays are fun, but it is in the silence after the upheaval that we find our footing again. Life is all about that balance—the ups and downs, the celebrations and the daily rituals that sustain us. Like the darkness and the light, it is the contrast that makes us appreciate what we have.

Take a moment today, and on any other days during the year that follow a holiday or commotion, and be grateful for the quiet times that fall in between and help us keep our balance. Light a black candle and a white candle on a firesafe surface and say:

Joyous noise,

Peaceful silence.

Life is all about the balance.

May I find my own balance through them both.

Snuff out the candles when you're done.

Deborah Blake

Notes:

July 6
Tuesday

4th ♊

Color of the Day: Maroon
Incense of the Day: Geranium

Maiden to Mother to Crone

I was well through and done with the maiden life phase and into the mother phase before I discovered Wicca. Now, as a grandmother, I am experiencing the transition from mother to crone. In reality, these roles may not be as simple as the triad implies. At ninety-plus years old, my own mother is the genuine crone of our family. My daughter is no longer a maiden, but a young mother. My granddaughter is not yet a maiden.

Pause and reflect today on the particular phase of life you inhabit. Are you transitioning? If so, where would you place yourself on the path? Research those goddesses who are traditionally associated with maiden/mother/crone. Perhaps you will discover some new or obscure deity with which to align your stage in life. Call to Demeter:

Demeter, symbol of steadfast and patient motherhood, be by our side through all the phases of our lives, a reminder that maternal love is everlasting and encompasses all.

Emyme

July 7
Wednesday

4th ♊

Color of the Day: Brown
Incense of the Day: Bay laurel

Mid-Week Balance

Wednesday might seem so far from the weekend, but it's actually the midpoint of the week. While we often work big acts of balance-related magic on the equinoxes, we need not miss the weekly opportunity that Wednesday presents us for balance magic! Today, let's use Wednesday's energies to create a bit of balance for ourselves.

The tarot card associated with Wednesday is the Magician. Put the Magician card from your favorite tarot deck on your altar. This card actually is a wonderful image of power and balance. The Magician has all the elements at his disposal to handle situations in a balanced manner. Meditate on what it means to act with power but in balance. Use the strength gained from this knowledge to propel you through your tasks for the rest of the week.

Blake Octavian Blair

July 8
Thursday

4th ♊

☽ v/c 12:20 am

☽ → ♋ 9:51 am

Color of the Day: Purple
Incense of the Day: Jasmine

A Charm to Inspire Summer Projects

For many of us, summer is a joyful period of increased freedom. Many schools are on break, more people go on vacation, and even work atmospheres may feel more relaxed. Now is the perfect time to go on an adventure, find new romance, take up a new hobby, or otherwise spice up your life with the creative, fresh energy of the season.

To ensure that a new summer project is successful or to draw inspiration and adventure into your life, take a square of yellow fabric and place in the center a sprig of peppermint, some basil leaves, three shiny pennies, and a piece of citrine or clear quartz. Place your hands over the mixture and imagine yourself happy and optimistic. When you're ready, bring the ends of the fabric to the center and tie them with a piece of green string. Carry the charm in a pocket or in your purse.

Thorn Mooney

 July 9
Friday

4th ♋

New Moon 9:17 pm

Color of the Day: Coral
Incense of the Day: Violet

Renewal Spell

Try to get outside tonight if you can. If not, simply close your eyes and imagine you're gazing up at the dark sky. The new moon is a perfect time for starting projects or simply renewing any part of your life that needs a boost—maybe you'd like to restart an exercise program or look for a new job. This spell can be used anytime you need to refresh or prepare for a new adventure.

As you gaze up at the sky, consider how the moon moves through its phases. You're "new" right now as well—a tiny seed germinating in darkness. Chant these words:

The moon is new and so am I,

A sliver in the darkened sky.

All the cycles wax and wane,

For the balance they maintain.

Like the moon I'm starting slight,

But soon will grow both strong and bright.

Ember Grant

 July 10
Saturday

1st ♋

☽ v/c 12:10 pm

☽ → ♌ 8:21 pm

Color of the Day: Gray
Incense of the Day: Pine

A July Abundance Ritual

Now we're past the solstice. The hours of daylight dwindle, but it's still summer. The sun and earth provide us with food and plenty. This ritual helps us give thanks at this bountiful time of year.

Begin this ritual at sunset. Drape your altar with green or purple fabric. Place two purple candles on the altar, one for the sun and one for the earth. Place one glass of sweet red wine or grape juice on the altar as well. Safely light each candle, then say:

The Sun's rays begin to dim,

But still we honor him.

The Goddess blesses us with her yield.

Now we honor the bounty of the field.

Take one sip of wine or juice. Pour the remaining wine on the ground outside. Snuff out each candle one at a time. You may use the candles for other rituals. Think of this ritual as you shop for groceries.

James Kambos

July 11
Sunday

1st ♌

Color of the Day: Yellow
Incense of the Day: Marigold

Wrist Bath to Prevent Swooning

Many recipes designed to treat the hands and wrists for hot flashes have survived, from Mrs. Beeton's to Taoist medical teas. This particular one is a personal favorite. It works within fifteen to thirty seconds on most folks and will prevent heat stroke. Although soaking your hands a few times a day in ice cubes can be tedious, it is better than being drenched in sweat or dehydrated all day on account of nature and her wonderful little hormonal and weather-driven nuances. This recipe is most effective in hot climates and humid conditions and is also a great addition to lemonade and limeade. Enjoy!

Mix the following and freeze it into two ice cube trays for best effects. Enchant the mixture with any spoken spell as you see fit.

- 1 bunch fresh cilantro, minced
- 3 tablespoons honey
- 3 tablespoons grapefruit zest
- ½ cup lemon juice
- 1 cup water

- 12 crushed cardamom pods
- 6 drops tulsi (holy basil) essential oil

Estha McNevin

NOTES:

 July 12
Monday

1st ♈ ♌
☽ v/c 8:29 am

Color of the Day: Ivory
Incense of the Day: Hyssop

Find Your Tribe

Cicadas, also known as tree crickets, are a bug that represents transformation. Their loud, screeching songs can be heard in the summer in the Northern Hemisphere. They sing loudly in an effort to find a mate. They make a loud sound as a group to benefit everyone.

Use the wisdom of the cicadas to find more members of your magical tribe. Life is more meaningful when you find more of your own kind. If there are cicadas near where you live, go outside and say these words:

> The songs of the cicadas
> are loud and strong.
>
> When I stand together with
> others I can't go wrong.
>
> This nature music raises my vibe.
>
> I will work on finding more
> of my magical tribe.

You can utilize these words even without the songs of the cicadas. The message is the same. There is strength in numbers. Use this spell to reach out and find like-minded friends.

Sapphire Moonbeam

July 13
Tuesday

1st ♌

☽ → ♍ 4:30 am

Color of the Day: Scarlet
Incense of the Day: Ginger

Summertime Love Potion

This bright, summery potion can be drunk by a couple to enhance the loving feelings between the two of them or by an individual to infuse them with attractive vibrations while seeking a partner.

The usual method is to simmer the potion for ten to fifteen minutes over low heat in a cauldron, then strain into a pitcher. Empower each of the ingredients with your intention for love before adding it to the pot by holding your hands over the ingredient and visualizing love as you wish it to be. Add all of the following ingredients except the honey to a pot or cauldron, and simmer as directed. After the potion is strained, add the honey and stir. Drink either warm or cold.

- 2 teaspoons (or 2 tea bags) black tea or Earl Grey tea
- 1 teaspoon orange juice
- ½ teaspoon lemon juice
- ½ teaspoon mint
- Pinch nutmeg
- Pinch coriander
- 3 cups water
- 1 tablespoon honey

Michael Furie

NOTES:

July 14
Wednesday

1st ♍

Color of the Day: White
Incense of the Day: Honeysuckle

A Prayer to a Salamander

A salamander is a point of consciousness within the element of fire. When we tap into that consciousness, they can assist us in becoming invigorated and transformed.

For this spell you will need these materials:

- A piece of unlined paper
- A pen
- A fireplace or firepit (or a red candle in a firesafe cauldron)
- Some ground cinnamon

Write a prayer to a salamander for something that needs extra energy in your life. Then, at the peak of the sun, light a fire (or light the candle). Face south and imagine that the light and heat of the sun are permeating your skin. Contemplate the fire element. Imagine that you can perceive within the flame little beings dancing here and there. Maintain this imagery as you sprinkle some of the cinnamon over the flame as you chant seven times:

Burning bright,

The blazing light.

The flames that dance.

The flames empower.

Carefully burn the paper in the flames. Watch it burn away to ash, transformed by the fire.

Storm Faerywolf

NOTES:

July 15
Thursday

1st ♍

☽ v/c 2:46 am

☽ → ♎ 10:32 am

Color of the Day: Green
Incense of the Day: Carnation

Portable happy Place

We all have happy places here and there, outdoor spots that make us feel safe and peaceful. Maybe it's a favorite trail in a park, a childhood haunt, or an area of town that brings back happy memories. Next time you visit your own happy place, gather a little bit of dirt or some pebbles from the ground and put them in a tiny jar or envelope that you can carry.

Anytime you feel uneasy or overwhelmed, no matter where you are, pinch some of the earth from the jar or envelope between your fingers and rub them together. Focus on the movement of the grit against your skin and how it activates the peaceful vibrations in the dirt. Allow the vibrations to flow through the dirt, up your fingers, and all through your body in the form of calming white light.

You can do this anywhere, even in crowds, when you need a sense of calm.

Kate Freuler

 **July 16**
Friday

1st ♎

Color of the Day: Purple
Incense of the Day: Mint

A Simple Charm Bag for Clear Communication

Mercury is currently in Cancer, which means we will be speaking from our hearts and not our heads. This isn't always a bad thing; it will help some to finally open up. But those of us who are already emotionally inclined can expect things to be a little "extra" at this time. Cast this spell to ensure you are getting your point across during these emotional times.

In a small blue, purple, yellow, or silver pouch, put a large pinch each of dried rosemary, rose, alum, and rue. Take a loose piece of your hair and, if possible, tie a knot in it and then place that in the pouch. Tie the pouch together and keep it with you when needed.

Devin hunter

July 17
Saturday

1st ♎

2nd Quarter 6:11 am

☽ v/c 7:03 am

☽ → ♏ 2:38 pm

Color of the Day: Indigo
Incense of the Day: Sandalwood

Altar Blessing

An altar is a physical focus for magic and spirituality. It provides a place to work and worship. There is a distinction between things that change with each spell or ritual (such as stones to symbolize current astrological energies) and things that stay the same (like an offering bowl or incense burner). Other things such as divine icons or altar cloths may or may not change.

Here is a spell to bless the permanent tools on your altar. You will need your altar, your permanent tools, incense, sea salt, and a bowl of water.

First take everything off your altar and clean the top. Safely light the incense and sprinkle sea salt in the water. Invoke your patron deity(s). One at a time, place your permanent tools on the altar, each in its accustomed place. Hold each tool and say:

God/dess, bless this solid symbol of my faith. May it hold me securely and always support my work. So mote it be.

Waft incense smoke over the tool and sprinkle it with the salted water. Then place it on the altar.

Elizabeth Barrette

Notes:

Page 143

July 18
Sunday

2nd ♏

Color of the Day: Orange
Incense of the Day: Eucalyptus

Invocation for healing

Sundays are associated with the solar goddess Brigid, the Celtic goddess of hearth, home, healing, and inspiration. Today, invoke Brigid to ask for a bit of healing energy for those you know are in need of it and who desire such divine energy.

You will need a white candle and a chime, bell, or rattle. Optionally, include an image of Brigid (as a saint or goddess) or a Brigid's cross. Set the items up on your altar or as their own temporary altar. Safely light the candle and ring, chime, or rattle to announce your presence and begin your invocation. As you envision the glow of the candle as healing light, recite the following:

Lady of the flame,

Lady of healing,

Lady of the holy wells,

Lady Brigid!

On behalf of all who seek comfort,

*May we find your healing
power aflame in our souls.*

So mote it be!

Blake Octavian Blair

 July 19
Monday

2nd ♏
☽ v/c 12:30 pm
☽ → ♐ 5:08 pm

Color of the Day: Lavender
Incense of the Day: Lily

Summer Energy

The summer is at its height now, which makes this the perfect time to tap into the abundant energy of the season. This spell is best done outside in the light and warmth of the sun, but you can always sit inside in a sunny spot, or make do with your imagination if the weather isn't cooperating. Find a flower or herb that represents the energy of summer to you: a sunflower, some rosemary—whatever symbolizes the season to you. Hold it up to the sky and envision it pulling in all that power and energy. Then hold it to your chest and draw that energy inside as you say:

Glorious summer, warm and wonderful,

Fill me with your energy and power.

Deborah Blake

July 20
Tuesday

2nd ♐

Color of the Day: Red
Incense of the Day: Cedar

Dispel Your Anger

Magick is about empowerment and your ability to change your personal energy as well as influence events in your life. When your life unfolds in ways that make you unhappy, it is important to deal with your emotions. When anger arises, you need to find a way to work through it. Strong emotion needs to be felt, not pushed aside or ignored, so you can regain and maintain balance and harmony.

Write down the things in your life that make you angry, sad, or disappointed. Place the list in a metal bowl or cauldron. Use a match or lighter to carefully ignite the edge of the paper while it is inside the bowl or cauldron. Visualize the things you wrote on the paper while using the power of the fire to release and chant these words:

Release my anger,
disappointment, and sorrow.

I will not carry it into tomorrow.

Release my anger, set it free.

The only person it hurts is me.

Repeat these words and this spell until you feel that you have released the anger-filled emotions that no longer serve you.

Sapphire Moonbeam

NOTES:

July 21
Wednesday

2nd ♐

☽ v/c 6:26 pm

☽ → ♑ 6:36 pm

Color of the Day: Topaz
Incense of the Day: Marjoram

Travel to Salem

Where do you live? Where do you vacation? Where I live, this time of the year is edging toward uncomfortably hot, and it is a very good time to go north to cooler climes. Salem, Massachusetts, is such a location and a terrific place to visit and review our heritage. Be prepared for a lot of kitsch and camp. Visit the museums and have your picture taken flying on a broom or stirring a cauldron. While there are indeed shops there owned by genuine earth-based believers, with legitimate supplies, keep in mind that much of it is for the tourist trade. That is not to say you cannot enjoy the atmosphere. Enjoy the lighthearted fun!

Emyme

 ## July 22
Thursday

2nd ♑

☉ → ♌ 10:26 am

Color of the Day: Crimson
Incense of the Day: Clove

Cool It Down and Bring Balance

With the excitement that summer always seems to bring, it's easy for life to start feeling a little out of whack. School and work schedules change, festival and vacation season is in full swing, the days are getting hot, and many of us are busier than ever with travel, wrangling kids, or pursuing summer projects. Are you neglecting your self-care at this time of year? To cool down a bit and create the space to recenter yourself, fill a bowl with ice cubes (crushed ice is okay, too) and place it before you on your altar or table. Hold some of the ice in your hands if it's not too cold for you. Concentrate on the stillness and coolness of ice. Draw that stillness into yourself while saying:

Cool the fire,

Feel the chill.

Summer burns,

But I am still.

Allow the ice in the bowl to melt, and add it to your bathwater, or wash your face and hands with it, to fully draw its energy into you.

Thorn Mooney

July 23
Friday

2nd ♑

☽ v/c 12:34 pm

☽ → ♒ 8:12 pm

Full Moon 10:37 pm

Color of the Day: Rose
Incense of the Day: Alder

Eleven, Eleven

Today is the 204th day of the year and the 23rd day of the month of July. By using a bit of numerology, we arrive at the master number eleven. Many people view the number eleven as an activation number for spiritual enlightenment.

For this rite, you'll need a white candle in a fireproof container, a black cloth, and eleven stones or crystals.

At nightfall, place your candle in the fireproof container in the center of the black cloth. Place your eleven stones in a circle around the candle. Say:

By the light of the moon,

By the power of night,

By the number eleven,

My dreams and wishes take flight.

Allow the candle to safely burn down. Place the stones on your altar or in a special place where they can remind you of the power of the full moon and the number eleven.

Najah Lightfoot

 July 24
Saturday

3rd ♒

Color of the Day: Blue
Incense of the Day: Magnolia

Closure Spell

We all have things we need to resolve from time to time—issues or relationships we need to let go of. To help yourself move on from a difficult situation, collect the following items: a black candle and dish to burn it in, something to symbolize the situation (a photo or written description), and a pinch of black salt. Place the candle in the container and set it on top of the picture or written description. Sprinkle the salt in the container around the candle. As you light the candle, visualize the situation being resolved; see yourself letting it go. Chant these words as many times as you feel is necessary:

Let go, move on, be strong.

You may burn the photo or paper in the container with the candle if you wish. Allow the candle to burn out safely, then discard it.

Ember Grant

July 25
Sunday

3rd ♒

☽ v/c 7:14 pm

☽ → ♓ 11:30 pm

Color of the Day: Gold
Incense of the Day: Frankincense

Break a Hex Spell

Mint and pepper team up in this spell to break a hex. Just combine three leaves chopped fresh mint (or two teaspoons dried mint) and a teaspoon black pepper in a small bowl. After dark, sprinkle the mixture outside your front and back doors. Before you begin, read this aloud:

When you feel you've been hexed,

No need to fear or feel vexed.

Without harm, none will you injure.

But this spell you must conjure.

Then, with a bit of pepper and a bit of mint, announce in the dark your magical intent:

Mint, heal, and pepper, sting.

No curse shall cross this protective ring!

After you've finished, go inside, slam your door, lock it, and say:

In these walls I'm protected as can be,

From curse, foe, or any who don't carry my key!

You're done.

James Kambos

July 26
Monday

3rd ♓

Color of the Day: White
Incense of the Day: Clary sage

Sprouting Wealth

The last half of summer really is a powerhouse of life and fertility. Capturing that energy for our wallet and purse magick is as simple as sprouting clover seeds.

In a large glass loaf pan, soak a half cup of clover seeds and three one-dollar bills in a half cup of water. Poke holes in the money or tear the edges to give the plants something to hold onto. Nestle this in a warm and sunny location and watch the life grow!

For twelve days, carefully drain the old water while holding back the seeds and dollar bills. Each day, replace it with fresh water until the seeds sprout. Once full leaves begin to form, plant this cluster of clovers in a container or out in the garden to generate greater wealth within and all around your home. Add coins and precious stones to create places where these buried treasures can help improve and generate auspicious vibrations.

Estha McNevin

July 27
Tuesday

3rd ♓

☽ v/c 9:13 pm

Color of the Day: Gray
Incense of the Day: Cinnamon

Magical Blemish Removal

A classic technique for getting rid of things such as warts and pimples is to rub each one with a small piece of meat, a bean, or a slice of potato and bury the pieces in the ground during a waning moon. This method can still be used today, and with the sun in the beauty-conscious sign of Leo and the moon waning in Pisces, it is an ideal time.

To begin, gather as many bits of the food options as you need, and rub one on each blemish, setting the bits in a bowl afterward. Once finished, go to a spot outdoors and bury them in the earth. As the pieces are buried, say the following three times:

As these portions rot and decay,

*So blemishes shall dissolve
and fade away.*

Then walk away from the burial spot without looking back.

Michael Furie

July 28
Wednesday

3rd ♓

☽ → ♈ 5:58 am

Color of the Day: Yellow
Incense of the Day: Lavender

House Naming and Altar

To animists, everything is alive. This includes our homes. Your home is your sacred space, so take a moment today to recognize that it has a spirit all its own.

If you have not already done so, come up with a fitting name for your home, then create a simple altar to the spirit of your home. This can be as simple as a candle upon the mantel or a rock from your yard in the corner of a kitchen counter that you keep an offering bowl upon. It need not be elaborate. I like to keep a bell in this sacred space as well. Ring the bell, light a candle, and declare aloud your home's new name—and use it often! Be sure to extinguish the candle.

Blake Octavian Blair

 July 29
Thursday

3rd ♈

Color of the Day: Turquoise
Incense of the Day: Nutmeg

Puddle Banishing Spell

Sometimes the most ordinary things are magical. For example, the fact that puddles of rainwater evaporate and change form after a storm, rising back into the sky as invisible vapor, is pretty amazing. A natural phenomenon like this is a perfect tool in magic.

For this spell you will need a pinch of salt, an ice cube tray and some water, and a puddle of rainwater that you know will dry up eventually.

When a problem is weighing heavy on your mind, hold the pinch of salt in your hand. Send your negative thoughts into the salt, visualizing it becoming gray and murky with unwanted energy. Now place the salt in one square of the ice cube tray. Fill the square with water and freeze.

Next time it rains and puddles form outdoors, retrieve your ice cube. Choose a puddle and place the ice cube in it. Imagine how, over the next few days, the ice cube will melt into water and then the water will transform into vapor, disappearing into the air. As the puddle dries up in the sun, so should your problem be resolved.

Kate Freuler

 July 30
Friday

3rd ♈

☽ v/c 3:38 pm
☽ → ♉ 4:08 pm

Color of the Day: Pink
Incense of the Day: Violet

Friendship Magic

Today is International Day of Friendship. Devote some time to your relationships. Each relationship is like a bank account. When you do nice things for a friend, you deposit energy in the account. When you ask for favors or make mistakes, you withdraw energy from the account. A healthy relationship should have a well-balanced give-and-take of energy.

Gather together some polished rose quartz pebbles, a stone of friendship. Name each stone for someone special in your life. Meditate on your relationship with each person as you hold their stone. How balanced is your relationship? Have you done too much for it, or too little?

Most relationships can benefit from investing more energy in them. To improve the balance, choose several small actions or one larger action to perform. Carry the stone(s) with you until you feel that you have balanced that relationship. You may give the stones to your friends or cleanse the stones and put them back in your working tools.

Elizabeth Barrette

July 31
Saturday

3rd ♉
4th Quarter 9:16 am

Color of the Day: Brown
Incense of the Day: Ivy

Stones of Protection

To make these protective stones, you will need the following materials:

- Several medium to large-size rocks
- A lemon
- A large bowl of water
- Some sea salt
- A towel
- Acrylic paint
- A paintbrush

Collect several medium to large-size rocks. These can be collected on your walks or even purchased from a garden store. Gather them, along with the other materials. Cut the lemon in half and squeeze the juice of one half into the bowl of water, then sprinkle in some salt. Wash each stone lovingly in the water while continuously chanting this verse:

Stone of protection,

Stone of defense.

Towel the stones dry and then paint upon each one a symbol of power while continuing the same chant the whole time. These symbols can be common ones, like a pentagram, triquetra, or hamsa, or they may be sigils of your own creation.

Once all have been painted, place each stone outside your home to create a protective circle.

Storm Faerywolf

August

S ummer is at its height of power when August rolls in, bringing with it the first of the harvest festivals, Lughnasadh (or Lammas), on the first of the month. Lughnasadh is a festival of strength and abundance, a reflection of August itself. Lugh and the Corn God are highly celebrated during this month and are particularly good to work with in spells or rituals for abundance, prosperity, agriculture, marriage, or strength. The Earth Mother in her many forms is ripening and overflowing with abundance. While we often see the first harvest as being associated with corn, there is much more that has been harvested by this point. We must remember not to overlook anything or take anything for granted in our lives, and the harvest is an excellent reminder of that. It is a time to begin focusing on expressing appreciation and giving thanks for all that we have.

The full moon this month is most often called the Corn Moon, but also goes by the Wyrt Moon, Barley Moon, or Harvest Moon. The stones carnelian, fire agate, cat's eye, and jasper will add extra power to your spells and rituals at this time. Use the herbs chamomile, St. John's wort, bay, angelica, fennel, rue, barley, wheat, marigold, or sunflowers in your spells. The colors for August are yellow, gold, and the rich green of the grass and leaves.

Kerri Connor

August 1
Sunday

4th ♉

Color of the Day: Yellow
Incense of the Day: Hyacinth

Lammas

First Fruits

Lughnasadh has roots in Irish mythology and legend as a festival in honor of the god Lugh. This day has come to be celebrated in many ways, including acknowledging the first harvest. Create your own First Fruits blessing by buying some local produce today or, even better, harvest from your own garden if you can. Any type of food item can be used for the blessing—fruit, vegetable, grain, or herb. After you've selected your item to symbolize the harvest, decorate your altar with seasonal items and candles. Place your "first fruit" in the center and chant this blessing for abundance:

Bless this harvest, Earth sustain us, flower, fruit, and grain.

Bring abundance, Earth maintain us, blessed be our gain.

Ember Grant

 August 2
Monday

4th ♉

☽ v/c 3:41 am
☽ → ♊ 4:46 am

Color of the Day: Gray
Incense of the Day: Hyssop

Peridot Abundance Spell

The birthstone for the month of August is peridot. In ancient Egypt peridot was held in high esteem by the pharaohs, and it is still considered the national gem of Egypt today. Peridot is associated with joy and light and is known as the "gem of the sun."

In order to increase all forms of abundance in your life, place a peridot gemstone on your altar or sacred space. Surround the peridot with coins to symbolize monetary gain. Visualize the abundance that you want in your mind's eye and see the light radiating from the gemstone outward to the coins. Take a deep breath and chant these words to manifest what you desire:

I am grateful for the prosperity I have today.

I ask that more abundance come my way.

Sapphire Moonbeam

August 3
Tuesday

4th ♏ ♊

Color of the Day: White
Incense of the Day: Basil

Bubble Magick

Is something troubling you, bothering your heart? Then float it away in this magickal childhood art.

Close up your troubles in a bubble and watch them disappear. Gaze upon the multicolored rainbows that brighten a bubble and cleanse your tears and soothe your fears.

Bubbles are magickal; they only exist for a while. Where they eventually float away to we can only guess, but in our imagination, their existence is limitless.

Today, buy yourself a bottle of bubbles. When life gets too heavy or things have you down, blow yourself a bubble and remember magick is always around.

Watch your bubbles float away, and embrace the bubble magick you created today.

Najah Lightfoot

August 4
Wednesday

4th ♏ ♊

☽ v/c 3:38 pm

☽ → ♋ 5:17 pm

Color of the Day: Topaz
Incense of the Day: Bay laurel

Dawn Prayers to Ra

Celebrate the sun as it rises today by breathing in the light and letting the hands of God fill your naked body in the sunlight. In a private or skyclad-friendly environment, find some time to let it all hang out. Love your body with frankincense lotion, and burn Egyptian incense to enable light to reach all of your nooks and crannies. Take stock of your body's strengths and weaknesses, and apply yourself to healthful habits as you work toward the harvest season under the watchful eye of Ra. May this prayer inspire you to truly know thyself. Declare it aloud six times:

Light, like a hand, descends to touch what it has created.

Ra, like a father, breathes life into me, loves my every breath, and sees me in my completion.

Light wills life to infinity.

Estha McNevin

August 5
Thursday

4th ♋

Color of the Day: Green
Incense of the Day: Jasmine

Eye of the Tiger Courage Charm

For this charm you will need a small piece of tiger's eye. This can be a tumbled stone or a piece of jewelry.

Hold the stone in your projective hand (i.e., the one you would normally use to throw a ball), holding it to your solar plexus. Imagine that all of your attention and energy is being focused into the stone in the form of a warm golden light. Call up the image of a tiger before you. Use all of your senses to make it seem more real. Imagine the soft fur and the strength of the tiger's muscles. Repeat three times:

> Though I may fear,
>
> The tiger is near.
>
> To keep clear my sight,
>
> Each day and each night.

Keep the stone with you. When you find yourself dealing with fear, touch the stone and remember the golden light within it.

Storm Faerywolf

August 6
Friday

4th ♋
☽ v/c 6:12 pm

Color of the Day: Purple
Incense of the Day: Mint

Home Blessing Spray

Smoke ceremonies to bless and cleanse the home are very popular nowadays, but what if you don't like all that smoke? If you have sensitive lungs or just don't like the smell, an easy alternative is to create your own room spray with water and a few essential oils.

This spray is meant as a general positive energy booster. It can be used to uplift the mood in your home, clear out bad vibes after a disagreement, and keep your house smelling fresh.

Gather these materials:

- 3 drops pine oil
- 3 drops sage oil
- 3 drops peppermint oil
- 1 small tumbled quartz crystal
- A small spray bottle (available at dollar stores)
- Water to fill the bottle

Place the oils, crystal, and water into the spray bottle and cap tightly.

Take the bottle to a warm, sunny spot and hold it up so the rays are touching it. Say:

Blessings and happiness,
safe and sound,

My home is a place where
good vibes abound.

Spray around the house as needed. Don't spray directly onto furniture or textiles, as it may stain.

Kate Freuler

NOTES:

August 7
Saturday

4th ♋

☽ → ♌ 3:31 am

Color of the Day: Blue
Incense of the Day: Rue

Lighthouse Protection Spell

Today is National Lighthouse Day. A lighthouse is both a form of communication and an aid to travelers. It marks a dangerous stretch of shore so ships can avoid it. That makes it ideal as a symbol of protection.

For this spell you will need a lighthouse. It can be a pendant, key chain, hair clip, belt buckle, picture, or any other item you can carry easily. You will also need a recording of a foghorn and the surf to play during the ritual. Any lighthouse and beach will do for the recording. Finally, you will need some salt and a bowl of water.

First turn on the sound and listen to the foghorn and the waves. Hold your lighthouse image in your hand. Concentrate on its purpose and say:

Lighthouse, keep me safe from unseen
shoals and other hazards as I travel.

Mix the salt into the water and sprinkle the lighthouse with it. Say:

Following your guidance keeps
me safe through the storms.

Carry your lighthouse whenever you travel.

Elizabeth Barrette

August 8
Sunday

4th ♌

New Moon 9:50 am

Color of the Day: Amber

Incense of the Day: Almond

Islamic New Year begins at sundown

Self-Care Spell

Today is the new moon in Leo, and by harnessing the power present today, we can reinforce a strong sense of self-esteem. For this spell, all that's needed is a gold candle. Upon waking but before getting ready for the day, hold the candle in your dominant hand and squeeze it gently while visualizing a glittering beam of sunlight shining down and filling the candle with power. Infuse into this the idea that this magic will strengthen your resolve to always take proper care of yourself and that you will always have a gentle air of royalty about you. Now light the candle and say:

Sun and moon and Leo combine,

Charge my life with strength and grace;

*Filled with intention and
resolve to remind*

To grant myself my rightful place.

Leave the candle burning (if safe) while you get ready, ideally on the bathroom sink while grooming. Then extinguish it and continue on with your day.

Michael Furie

 August 9
Monday

1st ♌

☽ v/c 8:23 am

☽ → ♍ 10:56 am

Color of the Day: Ivory

Incense of the Day: Rosemary

Cut and Clear Spell

The moon enters Virgo today, giving us time to take inventory of the people and projects we have been investing in. Are those investments worthwhile and making you feel fulfilled? If not, it might be time to let them go! Cast this simple cut and clear spell when it is time to cut the ties to that which does not serve you.

Write your name on the center of a white piece of paper. Around your name, write about the people and situations that need to go in as much detail as possible. Fill the whole sheet with everything that is bothering you. Next, anoint a pair of scissors with lemon, orange, tea tree, or eucalyptus oil and say:

In the name of all that is true,

I cut my ties to you!

Now cut out your name from the center of the paper. Carefully burn the remaining pieces in a cauldron, fireplace, or bonfire to banish their influence. Put the piece with your name on it in your book of shadows.

Devin Hunter

August 10
Tuesday

1st ♍

Color of the Day: Red
Incense of the Day: Ylang-ylang

Fresh from the Garden

One of the best things about this time of year is the abundance of fresh fruits and vegetables. If you have a garden, you are beginning to reap the bounty of your labors, but even if you don't, there are farmers' markets and CSAs (community-supported agriculture, where people buy a share of a farmer's crop and receive a box of seasonal produce throughout the harvest season). Many grocery stores carry local produce, too. Whether you grow it yourself or simply enjoy what others have grown, remember that in eating fresh food, we connect not only with nature but also with all our ancestors who took joy in this abundance. Rather than taking it for granted, set aside a few minutes in every meal to eat mindfully, with gratitude for nature's gifts. Go out of your way to include fresh produce in your diet, and don't forget to say thank you!

Deborah Blake

August 11
Wednesday

1st ♍

☽ v/c 7:22 am
☽ → ♎ 4:08 pm

Color of the Day: Brown
Incense of the Day: Lilac

Time Stands Still Meditation

If there is ever a moment when time could stand still, it's on an August afternoon. The wind doesn't stir and the streams are silent as they dream of May. In the late afternoon the cicadas sing lazily in the August heat.

August afternoons are a perfect time to scry and meditate. You'll need a smooth rock that appeals to you. You'll also need a calm body of water. This could be a lake, pond, or birdbath. A bowl of water may also be used; however, try to perform the meditation outside.

Hold your rock and sit before the body of water. Ground and center. When ready, drop your rock into the water. Watch the ripples move in outward circles, like time itself. Do you see any images? Just let them come. Don't try to figure them out. The answers will come to you later. Relax and return to your everyday state of mind.

James Kambos

August 12
Thursday

1st ♎

Color of the Day: Turquoise
Incense of the Day: Clove

Magickal Jam

Different berries have various magickal associations, just like flowers and herbs do. This means you can eat the berries on their own and bring their qualities into your life, or you can consume them year-round in the form of delicious jam. You can make your own jam or buy it ready-made at the grocery store or farmers' market.

Toast a piece of bread with your breakfast. Using a spoon, place the jam onto the toast in a shape representing what you'd like to attract that day, such as a heart for love, an arrow for courage, or a dollar sign for money. As you eat your toast, imagine yourself being filled with the energy of your chosen jelly, whether it's joy, love, or protection. The qualities of the berries will stay with you throughout your day.

Here are some jams and jellies to try:

- *Blueberry:* Protection, warding off psychic attack
- *Blackberry:* Healing, wealth
- *Strawberry:* Love, romance
- *Cherry:* Relationships, emotional connections
- *Raspberry*: Protection from spirits
- *Currant:* Health
- *Gooseberry:* Youth, beauty
- *Grape:* Fertility, mental clarity
- *Elderberry:* Prosperity, blessings

Kate Freuler

Notes:

August 13
Friday

1st ♎

☽ v/c 4:39 pm

☽ → ♏ 8:01 pm

Color of the Day: White
Incense of the Day: Thyme

Making Magical Ink

A great way to augment the power of your magical record keeping or journaling is by making your own inks. Not only is this a fun way to get crafty, but it's also relatively easy! For this recipe, you'll need a mortar and pestle, a bowl, a piece of cheesecloth, one teaspoon white vinegar, a funnel (optional), and a clear, clean jar. You'll also need to collect two cups of berries. I love pokeweed for this because it's a common wild plant, growing in most regions of the continental United States, and it's bearing fruit at this time of year. You can use many kinds of berries, however, so use what you have.

To begin, smash the berries to a pulp using the mortar and pestle. Then strain the pulp by pouring the concoction through cheesecloth, allowing the juice to collect in a clean bowl. Add the white vinegar and stir. Use a funnel (or just a very steady hand) to transfer your finished ink into the jar for storage. You can use your ink with a dip pen, a quill, or a paintbrush.

Thorn Mooney

August 14
Saturday

1st ♏

Color of the Day: Gray
Incense of the Day: Magnolia

Bless My Animal Companions

I live as part of a pack, with two cats and a dog. Their unconditional love is a source of powerful healing and magic. I feel loved and know I belong.

If, like me, you are part of a pack, regularly bless your animal companions. The energy will surround them and help dispel adversity, protecting your animal allies.

Get collars for your animals. Put bells on cat collars so that birds and chipmunks are warned that the fierce hunters are coming. Dog tags can be attached to dog collars.

Each morning, take time to ritualistically put the collar on the animal, and say:

I bless you with love and light that you may be safe, always find your way home, and know you are loved.

At night, when all of the animals return to the house, I remove their collars and give thanks for their health.

Dallas Jennifer Cobb

August 15
Sunday

1st ♏︎

2nd Quarter 11:20 am

☽ v/c 11:05 pm

☽ → ♐︎ 11:12 pm

Color of the Day: Gold

Incense of the Day: Juniper

A Penny for Prosperity

Bury a penny either in the ground or in a potted plant (if that's all you have available). If possible, find a penny minted in the year you were born. Say these words as you bury it:

*I know that it's worth far
more than a cent.*

I offer the earth this coin with intent.

Visualize the prosperity you need to reach your goals and be successful.

Ember Grant

 August 16
Monday

2nd ♐︎

Color of the Day: Silver

Incense of the Day: Lily

Moonstone Travel Safety Magic

Monday's lunar ties connect it with moonstones, making this a perfect day to do a little crystal magic! One of the many magical uses for moonstone is to promote safe travel. Find a moonstone and a small pouch. Cleanse the crystal and pouch as you see fit, then hold them cupped in your hands. Visualize a protective glowing light radiating from the stone, and recite the following:

Lunar powers shining bright,

Combining with earthen crystal might.

I perform this magical rite.

May I have safe travels day and night.

Now, holding your intention and using your breath, blow your intention into the stone in your cupped hands. Then put the stone in the pouch and tuck it somewhere safe in your vehicle. Over time, as you feel called, you can also add magical plants to the pouch that add to your travel safety magic, such as pine needles for protection or lavender for calm.

Blake Octavian Blair

August 17
Tuesday

2nd ♐

☽ v/c 9:43 pm

Color of the Day: Maroon
Incense of the Day: Cedar

Scratches and Stings

Today we pay homage to two benign beasts that are unquestionably important to Wiccan life: the black cat and the honey bee.

Black cats are said to be the age-old popular companions to witches. Whether this is true or not, let us show our appreciation for them with the blessing below, which can be adapted for your own cat or modified for use with any other familiar.

Honey bees are absolutely necessary for our survival. No bees means less food and darn few flowers. Few flowers and plants leads to a scarcity of ingredients for potions and spells. The honey bee population worldwide has been in danger for years. Take a few minutes today to send positive energy to the honeybee with this blessing.

Bastet, lover of cats, and Neith,
keeper of bees, we call upon you to
always protect your chosen beings,
which bring joy and sustenance,
happiness and health, to our lives.

Emyme

August 18
Wednesday

2nd ♐

☽ → ♑ 1:58 am

Color of the Day: White
Incense of the Day: Honeysuckle

Lovely Limoncello

Its origins are steeped in mystery, and its ingredients are deceptively simple: lemons, grain alcohol, water, and sugar. Whether you make your own limoncello or buy it in a store, the golden yellow liquid will cool your throat and lift your spirits.

For this spell you will need:

- A yellow candle
- Fireproof candleholder
- A saucer
- One lemon cut into slices
- Ice-cold limoncello
- Shot glasses

Place your yellow candle in the candleholder. Set the candle on the saucer. Arrange the lemon slices around the candle. Pour limoncello into the glasses. Light the candle and say:

Golden light, summer bright,

Yellow lemons, my delight.

Limoncello, sweet and tasty,

We raise our glasses and toast to thee!

Be sure to extinguish the candle.

Najah Lightfoot

 August 19
Thursday

2nd ♑

☽ v/c 7:59 pm

Color of the Day: Crimson
Incense of the Day: Carnation

The Little Ocean

This spell is for getting more in touch with the water element. You will need these materials:

- Your bath or shower
- A dark blue or black candle
- A handful of sea salt
- A large bowl of water

Draw a bath. (If you're using a shower, skip to the next step.) Ground and center. Safely light the candle. Add the handful of salt to the bowl of water and swirl it with your fingers, imagining it like a little ocean. Gently slosh the water from side to side, imagining the great tides of the sea now symbolically reflected in this bowl of salt water. Say:

The ebb and flow,

The rise and fall,

I sail over the starry seas.

Pour the water into the bath or over your head as you step into the shower. Imagine yourself communing with the powers of water, floating in the ocean

or out in a rainstorm. When you are done, extinguish the candle and save it for your next magical bath.

Storm Faerywolf

NOTES:

 August 20
Friday

2nd ♑

☽ → ♒ 4:49 am

Color of the Day: Pink
Incense of the Day: Violet

Rule of Three Gratitude Spell

Gratitude is an important life skill. By focusing on what we have, we increase our awareness and satisfaction. We also become more mindful of those who have less. That encourages us to clean house and remove what we don't use.

This spell utilizes practical action to harness the Rule of Three: that which you do comes back to you three times over. Sort through your bookcase for books you don't read. Check your cabinets for dishes or other items you don't need. Pack them up to take to a thrift store, a garage sale, a giveaway, etc. For every bundle of stuff that you send out of your home, name something that you feel grateful for. Concentrate on that sense of gratitude. Then say:

I release these things that I no longer
need in order to make room for more
that I can use. I express my gratitude
for unknown blessings yet to come.

Elizabeth Barrette

August 21
Saturday

2nd ♒

Color of the Day: Indigo
Incense of the Day: Sandalwood

Strength to Overcome Obstacles

Gladiolus is the flower for the month of August. Gladiolus flowers represent strength and the ability to overcome obstacles. They bloom in a variety of colors, like red, pink, white, yellow, and orange.

Anything that symbolizes strength can help you become more empowered. Empowerment is a key element in gaining confidence to overcome challenges on our spiritual path. Use the magick of the gladiolus to move forward after the lesson of the challenge or difficulty has been learned. While holding the flower, chant these words:

May the beauty and strength of
this gladiolus flower assist me
with its natural power, guide my
path, and allow me to see how
the obstacles can be overcome.

Say the words as many times as needed until you feel your inner strength rise and you have the confidence to move past the difficulty in your life.

Sapphire Moonbeam

August 22
Sunday

2nd ♒

☽ v/c 8:02 am

Full Moon 8:02 am

☽ → ♓ 8:43 am

☉ → ♍ 5:35 pm

Color of the Day: Orange
Incense of the Day: Heliotrope

Full Moon Spell for Thankfulness

Tonight, the August full moon, sometimes called the Grain Moon, will illuminate the sky. This moon will rise above an earth that is ripe and ready to be harvested. Decorate your altar with the bounty of the season. A vase of zinnias or black-eyed Susans would be nice. A few stems of grain and some ears of corn would also be appropriate.

Tonight's ritual should be about giving thanks. Safely light a gold pillar candle on your altar. Meditate about the good things in your life. On a sheet of stationery, write a sentence or two about one thing you are grateful for. Let the candle burn for a few minutes, then extinguish it. Leave the stationery on your altar for three days, then discard it. Use the candle again for thankfulness or wealth spells. Expect other good things to come your way. The divine appreciates your gratitude.

James Kambos

August 23
Monday

3rd ♓

Color of the Day: White
Incense of the Day: Neroli

harness the Power of Virgo

As you probably already know, the sun is now in Virgo! This season is a monthlong celebration of sassiness, organization, and accomplishing big goals. Even if you aren't a Virgo, you can still tap into this energy at any time. Here is a spell that will allow you to do just that.

Take a piece of carnelian, citrine, moss agate, or jade and charge it in the sun all afternoon. Just before the sun goes down, take the stone in your hands, kiss it, and say:

Warmed by the burning sun,
charged by the will of one.

Channel the Virgo vibration, solid
and strong regardless of the station!

Keep the stone with you or on your altar, and use it in your workings when you need a bit of extra juju over the next month.

Devin hunter

 ## August 24
Tuesday

3rd ♓

☽ v/c 5:12 am
☽ → ♈ 2:57 pm

Color of the Day: Gray
Incense of the Day: Bayberry

Gifts for the Faeries

No one really knows what faeries are, other than that they almost certainly aren't the cute little winged creatures you see in a Disney movie. Most Witches believe that they are a form of elemental. Just because most of us never see one doesn't mean they aren't there. The fae, or fair folk, as they are sometimes called, should always be treated with respect and just a bit of caution. It never hurts to try to make friends with them. The summer, when flowers are blooming, is the perfect time to do this.

Find a spot in your yard or a park or field that looks like it might be a place that faeries would like, and bring them a gift. It is said that they like flowers, honey, mead, milk, and shiny things. Set down whatever gift you have brought, back away a few paces, and say:

A gift for the faeries, lovely and wise.

May it bring me favor in your eyes.

Deborah Blake

August 25
Wednesday

3rd ♈

Color of the Day: Yellow
Incense of the Day: Lilac

Boost a Spell

When you're waiting for a spell to manifest, give it a boost with this simple chant. Visualize things falling into place and burn some incense as you focus your intent on the original spell. Say:

I understand these things take time,

As the pieces fall in line.

To ensure success is mine,

Reinforce it with this rhyme.

Repeat these words anytime you find yourself thinking about your goal and you feel restless waiting for the results.

Ember Grant

 August 26
Thursday

3rd ♈

☽ v/c 5:14 pm

Color of the Day: Purple
Incense of the Day: Balsam

Sunflower Seed Divination

Here is an easy divination method using sunflower seeds to get an answer to a simple yes-no question.

You will need a stick for drawing on the ground and some sunflower seeds. Gather the same number of seeds as your current age.

Use the stick to draw a line about a yard long on the ground. On the right side of the line, carve the word "yes," and on the left side write "no." Now turn your back on the line, and stand with it directly behind you, with one end at your feet.

Hold the sunflower seeds in both hands and ask your question.

Throw them back over your head and let them land where they may. Turn around and count how many landed on each side of the line. The side with the most seeds is your answer.

If you do this in a rural or private setting, you can leave the seeds for the wildlife to eat. Otherwise clean them up.

Kate Freuler

August 27
Friday

3rd ♈

☽ → ♉ 12:27 am

Color of the Day: Rose
Incense of the Day: Cypress

A Self-Love Letter

Fridays are associated with the Norse goddess Freya, who rules over battle but also love and sexuality. Whether or not you're in a relationship, it's always worth taking time to practice a little self-love.

Today, write yourself a love letter to save for when you're feeling down and need a boost of confidence. You may write this in any form you choose, but it's important that you be specific. Describe the qualities you like best about yourself. List the things you've overcome or accomplished, and offer yourself praise. Imagine the future and all of the things you hope for yourself, then encourage your future self to achieve those dreams. Address your letter to your future self from your past self. When you're done, seal your letter in an envelope addressed to you and say:

Sealed with love from me to me,

Kept for when it's time to see.

If I should feel lost or hurt,

Remind me of my own self-worth.

Keep your letter somewhere safe and open it when you need a boost.

Thorn Mooney

NOTES:

August 28
Saturday

3rd ♉

Color of the Day: Black
Incense of the Day: Sage

Charge Your Batteries

The last weekend of August is a great time to get outside. Can you take the day to go to a lake, river, stream, or ocean? Or visit a forest, mountain, or park? With recent attention to what is called nature deficit disorder, there is more and more research documenting the positive effects of nature on the human psyche and body.

While many of us live in cities, we can still find parkland, ravines, and cemeteries with large swatches of nature, wilderness, and greenery for us to connect to the sacred elements.

Take your lunch, a blanket, and a book. Lie down on the ground. (Earth.)

Breathe deeply.(Air.)

Feel the sun on your face or arms. (Fire.)

Wade, swim, or dip. (Water.)

Throughout the day, monitor the shift in your personal energy. Observe the positive effects of nature as it raises your vibration and charges your batteries. (Spirit.)

Dallas Jennifer Cobb

 August 29
Sunday

3rd ♉

☽ v/c 10:59 am

☽ → ♊ 12:42 pm

Color of the Day: Gold
Incense of the Day: Marigold

Mend a Broken Heart

How do you mend a broken heart? How do you know where to start? The best thing to do is to start working on yourself.

Gather some rose quartz crystals. The raw crystals are fine. In fact, they tend to have better energy than tumbled stones and crystals.

Sit in a cross-legged position or lie on the floor and get comfortable. Place the crystals around you in a circle pattern. Close your eyes and take several cleansing breaths. Concentrate on your heart and repeat these words as many times as needed:

I love myself, I will be good to me,

I fill my heart with love to set it free.

*After crying the tears from
my broken heart,*

*I will begin again with
a brand-new start.*

Love and peace begin with me,

My heart will mend, blessed be!

Sapphire Moonbeam

August 30
Monday

3rd ♊

4th Quarter 3:13 am

Color of the Day: Lavender
Incense of the Day: Narcissus

Calming Monday Vibes

For those who start their workweek on Monday, the day can bring a little apprehension and anxiety. Sometimes we need some reassurance to smooth out the emotional turbulence that can come with stress. Moonstone resonates with Monday's lunar energies and is the perfect stone for nerve-soothing magic at the top of the week!

Find a small moonstone that you can carry with you. Take a few minutes to sit calmly, holding it between your hands. Simply feel and mesh with its soothing energies. Let the stone speak to you through its energies. Let it communicate with you and share its energies through thoughts, feelings, and impressions. The stone people may speak softly, but it is in these ways that they communicate with us. Recite this simple enchantment:

Soothing moonstone, share with me

Your calming energies of stability.

Through the week, be with me,

Lending calm and cool, so mote it be.

Blake Octavian Blair

August 31
Tuesday

4th ♊

☽ v/c 4:48 pm

Color of the Day: Scarlet
Incense of the Day: Cinnamon

Magical Upcycling

What are your artistic, creative gifts? Are you skilled at cooking, painting, or fabric art? Whatever your gift, your crafting space is sure to hold at least one, if not several, items that have been recycled or upcycled. This could include inherited pots and pans, paintbrushes rescued from a yard sale, or vintage lengths of fabric bought at a thrift store. A couple of local artists I know collect costume jewelry and use it to fashion amazing picture frames. Another local crafter utilizes broken and discarded tile and glass in furniture and garden stones.

The presence and power of the previous owner lives on in the item. This can be a very good thing, or it may not be so welcome. Cleanse each item in an appropriate way, then request that the positive energy remain and the negative energy be banished. Rest assured that your appeal will be granted.

Emyme

September

The equinox happens toward the end of this month, heralding the beginning of autumn in the Northern Hemisphere and the start of spring in the Southern Hemisphere. An equinox happens when the sun crosses the celestial equator, an imaginary line in the sky not unlike our Earth's own equator. It's on the equinox that the sun rises due east and sets due west. This is why people often go to famous landmarks to watch the rising or setting of the sun on the equinoxes and solstices. In our ever-changing world, it's nice to know there are at least some constants!

Astrologically, the autumnal equinox is when the sun sign of Libra begins. It's fitting, as this is the time when day and night are of equal length, and Libra is the sign of the scales. The full moon that corresponds with this event is called the Harvest Moon or the Corn Moon. The few days around the equinox and the full moon bring a period in which everything is ripening and full of energy. It all seems to be coming into fullness, preparing either for the coming of winter or the start of the growing season.

Charlie Rainbow Wolf

September 1
Wednesday

4th ♊

☽ → ♋ 1:26 am

Color of the Day: Brown
Incense of the Day: Marjoram

Laughter for Our Spirit

Today is the birthday of actress and comedian Lily Tomlin, who is known for her portrayal of numerous quirky characters. It is well known that laughter is good for our health and improves our mood. Laughter feeds our spirit!

Today, spend some time watching a favorite comedian who always makes you laugh. Then learn a new joke that you can tell to friends to spread the joy and benefits of laughter. You can create your own joke or consult a book or website with jokes. Be sure to find one appropriate for your audience. Challenge the recipients of your comedic stylings to do the same: learn a joke and pass it on. You can turn your midweek blahs into a cascading pay-it-forward of mirth and laughter!

Blake Octavian Blair

September 2
Thursday

4th ♋

Color of the Day: Turquoise
Incense of the Day: Mulberry

Basket Blessing Wash

It's that time again to gather all of our baskets and begin filling them with fruits and veggies from the harvest! Sometimes our baskets don't look so great after a summer of heavy use in the garden. This wash cleans, disinfects, and seals the fibers of the baskets to help them last longer and withstand a bit more robust use. Rinsing them in a full tub of warm water is best, but some baskets like to be soaked overnight and will tolerate their weave being adjusted or mended after a dip in a solution made of the following ingredients:

- 3 tablespoons coconut-based soap, free & clear
- 12 drops essential tea tree oil
- 4 tablespoons pure almond oil
- 2 tablespoons sesame oil
- 4 cups distilled white vinegar
- 4 cups Everclear alcohol

May baskets and the art of weaving remind us of traditional pagan times, filling our homes with health, wealth, and a plentiful harvest. Envision these qualities when soaking your baskets in this helpful solution.

Estha McNevin

NOTES:

4th ♋

☽ v/c 1:37 am

☽ → ♌ 11:58 am

Color of the Day: Coral

Incense of the Day: Vanilla

hurry Up and Get Slow

Timing is everything. Sometimes we just need to slow things down in order to catch our breath.

For this spell you will need a pen or pencil, a thick, plain white paper plate, and a jar of molasses (or honey).

Think of something that you wish to slow down. Maybe it's a check that threatens to clear your account before payday, or how about a relationship that is going great but maybe just a bit too fast for your comfort.

On the paper plate, write down the thing that you wish to slow, or create a sigil to represent it. Slowly pour the molasses over it while repeatedly chanting in a low, slow almost-whisper:

Fast as a season for lovers apart,

Slow as molasses, slow as molasses.

Put the plate in your freezer until you no longer need to maintain influence over the issue, at which time you can bury the plate in a suitable place.

Storm Faerywolf

September 4
Saturday

4℞ ♌

Color of the Day: Gray
Incense of the Day: Patchouli

Embrace Learning

This is the time of year when kids go back to school and some folks are heading off to college. Whether or not you are attending any kind of formal classes, it is always good to keep learning. Learning new things helps your brain function, but it also makes you a more well-rounded person. And as Witches, we always want to be learning and growing as we practice our Craft.

Set a goal of learning one new thing every day, or every week, or every full moon. If you aren't someone to whom learning comes easily, feel free to ask for help. Sit with a book or your laptop (however you plan to find information), and focus on your desire to learn. Then say:

Athena, goddess of wisdom,

Help me to learn and grow.

Show me what I need to know.

Deborah Blake

September 5
Sunday

4℞ ♌

☽ v/c 10:22 am
☽ → ♍ 7:06 pm

Color of the Day: Yellow
Incense of the Day: Almond

Acorn Home Protection Spell

Oak trees are common throughout much of the US and Europe and have long been associated with wisdom, abundance, strength, longevity, and the changing season. Oak energy is deep and protective, and acorns are a great way to easily call upon that energy in your daily life.

For this spell, collect ten acorns. If you don't have access to acorns, you may choose other strong-feeling trees that are dropping nuts or fruits at this time of year and ask for their aid. Once you have collected ten, hold them in your hands and imagine a ring of protective trees growing strong around your home. Say:

My home is a fortress shielded in strength. Wisdom and love are abundant in this sacred grove, and all are protected from harm. So mote it be.

Bury the acorns in a ring around your property or apartment building (or even your whole town, if you want to go big!). You may also simply place them in the corners of your home or room, if your space is small.

Thorn Mooney

September 6
Monday

4th ♍

New Moon 8:52 pm

Color of the Day: White
Incense of the Day: Hyssop

Labor Day (US) –
Labour Day (Canada) –
Rosh hashanah begins at sundown

New Moon, New Job

The new moon is a space between the ending of one lunar cycle and the beginning of another. Things in life enter this phase and come out the other side reborn, just like the fresh waxing moon. This spell uses the transformative power of the new moon to create a job change or promotion.

Gather these items:

• A black bowl filled with water to represent the dark moon

• A waterproof object to represent your job (such as a paper clip, a nail, etc.)

After dark, sit outdoors or near a window with the bowl of water. Hold the object in your hand. Imagine your job as it is now and say:

Dark moon,

Cauldron of change,

I give this job to you.

Darkness stir,

Mysteries move,

Bring me something new.

Drop the object into the dark water and spend a moment visualizing yourself doing the job you want. Leave the water out overnight.

Dump the water onto the earth in the morning, and continue to use the object as change comes your way.

Kate Freuler

NOTES:

September 7
Tuesday

1st ♍

☽ v/c 3:24 pm

☽ → ♎ 11:20 pm

Color of the Day: Black
Incense of the Day: Geranium

Bless the hearth

Many believe that the hearth is the center of the home, and even if we aren't the best chefs in the world, the kitchen is an important part of life. Though house blessings are commonplace, a blessing specific to the kitchen and our modern hearth—the stove/oven—can be useful to keep the energy harmonious.

First, thoroughly clean the kitchen with the intention of removing physical grime and any psychic buildup as well. Then boil a mixture of water, sliced oranges (with the peel), and rosemary sprigs in a pot on the stove. As the mixture begins to steam and bubble, encircle your kitchen by moving clockwise in a circular motion while mentally sending loving energy through an athame or wand. As you circle, say:

*Filled with magic to transform
and combine, renewed and
empowered, this vital shrine.*

*Sacred hearth of this home, be
cleansed, be well, be blessed and warm.*

Michael Furie

September 8
Wednesday

1st ♎

Color of the Day: Topaz
Incense of the Day: Lavender

Forget a Lover Spell

At first you were in feel-it-to-your-toes love. But that was then. Your feelings have changed. This spell will help you forget 'em fast.

You'll need a tart apple, peeled. You'll also need some lemon juice and a crushed clove of garlic. Rub the lemon juice and garlic into the peeled apple. Rub it hard. Then set the apple on a paper towel to dry for a few days. It doesn't need to dry completely, but allow it to begin to shrivel. When the apple is ready, take it to a wooded area. Hold the apple, think of your former lover, and say:

I loved you at the start.

Now you're out of my mind—

And out of my heart!

End by throwing the apple as far as you can. Walk away. You can also throw the apple into the trash or a compost pile instead.

James Kambos

September 9
Thursday

1st ♍ ♎

Color of the Day: Purple
Incense of the Day: Apricot

Witch's Crown Spell

Today is full of air energy, with five planets in air signs. Expect lots of talking and to even find yourself in a debate or two. With the Moon, Mercury, and Venus in Libra right now, it's a good time to do magic that will restore balance to an area of your life where you have been feeling powerless. Cast this spell when you forget how good it feels to wear your crown.

Stand in front of a mirror. In the air before you, draw a pentacle with your index finger and say:

By balance, power, respect, awareness,
and divinity, I claim my crown in
the name of the witch's trinity!

Primal, ego, and higher soul, I summon
the crown and become whole!

Close your eyes, take a deep breath, and visualize a crown manifesting on your head.

Devin Hunter

 September 10
Friday

1st ♎

☽ v/c 12:48 am
☽ → ♏ 2:05 am

Color of the Day: Pink
Incense of the Day: Alder

Beauty Elixir

We all know that inner beauty is what counts, but it never hurts to look your best—especially for a special occasion. Keep in mind that an attitude of self-love is at the core of this spell. Know and see your true beauty and others will too.

Place a small piece of amber in a glass of cool water and let it soak for at least an hour. As you dress and prepare to go out, use this elixir to wash your face or add it to a bath. As you wash, repeat these words three times:

The more I love myself,
the more beautiful I'll be.

I will shine, I will glow—the
best of me is what they'll see.

Ember Grant

September 11
Saturday

1st ♏

Color of the Day: Indigo
Incense of the Day: Ivy

Day of Service

It's hard to believe it was twenty years ago on this date that the United States was attacked on its own soil. This has become a day of service and a reminder of the solidarity that was forged among citizens. It is a day that brings people together.

This date falling on a Saturday seems like a good time to seek out a local cause to which you can offer your time and talents. Should that not be an option for you, another option is to offer blessings to those allies without whose assistance we would all be living a different type of life:

*Lady and Lord, protect all nations
in all ways from darkness and evil.*

Emyme

 ## September 12
Sunday

1st ♏

☽ v/c 1:33 am
☽ → ♐ 4:34 am

Color of the Day: Amber
Incense of the Day: Juniper

Altar Renewal Spell

As summer wanes, our altars need renewal. Remove everything from your altar. Sort things into sacred tools and objects, supplies (like sage, sweetgrass, or salt), and seasonal objects and symbols.

Wipe down smooth surfaces, saying:

*May the grace of the Goddess
cleanse this altar.*

Place a fresh cloth upon your altar. Say:

*May the beauty of the
Goddess bless this altar.*

Place fresh candles in fireproof containers on the altar. Say:

*May the spirit of the Goddess
shine in all I do.*

Carefully place your magical tools. Say:

*May the sacred strength of the
Goddess live in all these tools.*

Create a container for all your supplies. Say:

> May the magic of the Goddess
> be in these elements.

House seasonal items separately, and take them out as needed. Whenever you work magic after this, light the candles, recall the renewal spell, and invoke:

> The grace, beauty, spirit, strength, and
> magic of the Goddess all live here.
> Dallas Jennifer Cobb

September 13
Monday

1st ♍ ♐
2nd Quarter 4:39 pm

Color of the Day: Lavender
Incense of the Day: Lily

Chocolate Meditation

September 13 is known as International Chocolate Day. In ancient times the Mayans and Aztecs used the base ingredient in chocolate during rituals to enhance their connection to the spirit world. Since chocolate releases endorphins that promote peaceful, loving feelings, meditating with chocolate can help you ease into the process.

Sit in a comfortable position and take three deep breaths. Place a small piece of chocolate in your mouth and let it melt onto your tongue. A more pure form of chocolate with less sugar is the most beneficial to connect you with spirit via meditation. As the chocolate slowly dissolves in your mouth, close your eyes and focus on going deep within while being mindful of the present moment. Relax and trust the guidance that you receive from your inner teacher and the wise whispers from your spirit guides.

Sapphire Moonbeam

September 14
Tuesday

2nd ♐

☽ v/c 6:57 am

☽ → ♑ 7:34 am

Color of the Day: Red
Incense of the Day: Basil

Summer Lovers

Love is in the air. The nights are warm and the stars are bright. There is laughter and romance in the night.

Your beloved may be with you or far away, or you may pine for love to come and stay.

On this night as the summer winds blow, become one with nature and watch your love grow.

Draw a bath or run a shower. Sprinkle rose petals in the water. Cup your hands and gently pour water over your head.

Acknowledge the healing, loving gentleness of water as it flows over your head and onto your body.

Cross your arms and hug yourself, for we must love ourselves first before we can love others. Visualize the love you desire.

Step from your bath and safely light a candle. Let it burn bright, and hopefully the love you seek will be in your dreams tonight!

Be sure to extinguish the candle.

Najah Lightfoot

September 15
Wednesday

2nd ♑

Color of the Day: Yellow
Incense of the Day: Bay laurel

Yom Kippur begins at sundown

Balance Meditation

Autumn is a time of balance. Light and dark, heat and cold, are moderated in this season. It's not just about balance in nature, though. It's also about balance within, work-life balance, and other personal aspects.

For this moving meditation, you will need a wobble board, a yoga ball, a bicycle, or another balance tool. First pay attention to your body. Think about how balanced you feel (or not). Climb onto your balance tool. Feel for your center of gravity. It should help you find your balance. Tilt your weight gently to feel the shifts, taking care not to fall off. Feel your awareness of gravity and your vertical axis. Visualize how the earth spins, always moving, always balanced. Think about different areas of your life. Are you doing too much of one thing and not enough of another? Feel how your balance shifts along with your thoughts. "Heavy" thoughts have weight! Imagine doing something different and see if that shifts your balance. After you finish meditating, go change one thing.

Elizabeth Barrette

September 16
Thursday

2nd ♑

☽ v/c 1:40 am

☽ → ♒ 11:23 am

Color of the Day: White
Incense of the Day: Nutmeg

The Cleansing Pool

Even if we don't think we need to do cleansing work, guess what? We do. We are receiving messages and energies each and every second of every day, and most of the time we are completely unaware of this. We need to periodically clear out these extraneous energies before they begin to fester. Think of it as spiritual and magical hygiene.

For this spell, gather these items:

• A white candle

• A large bowl of water

• Some sea salt

• Some fresh mint

Safely light the candle. Focus your awareness into the bowl of water. Imagine it is fresh and pure. Sprinkle a bit of salt into it, then crush and add some mint. Place your hands over the bowl, infusing it with life force, and say:

I conjure forth the crystal pool

With healing waters clear and cool.

Wash your face with the water, then your hands. Extinguish the candle and use it the next time you wish to perform this cleansing. Use the rest of the water to sprinkle around and/or outside your home.

Storm Faerywolf

NOTES:

September 17
Friday

2nd ♒

Color of the Day: Rose
Incense of the Day: Yarrow

Empress Card for Birthing Project Goals

We all have ideas for projects incubating in our minds. Here is some motivation magic to get them started! Find an image of the Empress card from your favorite tarot deck. The Empress represents fertility and bringing new life—qualities we want to home in on for our project. Gather a tealight candle and a carnelian stone. Put the image of the tarot card on your altar, and set the carnelian near the candle. (Make sure you burn the candle in a safe holder.) On a small piece of paper, write things you'd like to accomplish today to get your project started, even if they're small preliminary steps. Put your list under the candleholder and carnelian, then light the candle and visualize accomplishing your goal. Let the candle burn all the way down on its own, supervised and in a safe holder. When the candle is out, carry the charged carnelian with you for energetic oomph.

Blake Octavian Blair

September 18
Saturday

2nd ♒

☽ v/c 5:14 am
☽ → ♓ 4:22 pm

Color of the Day: Blue
Incense of the Day: Pine

Harvesting Prosperity

We are in the midst of the harvest season, which is a perfect time to work on magic for prosperity and abundance. You can use this simple spell at any time, but it is especially nice if you can do it either at noon in a patch of sunshine or during the full moon.

Take a pretty bowl and fill it with fresh fruits and/or vegetables. Make sure they are practically spilling out, to represent the abundance of the season. Place your hands around the sides of the bowl and feel all that fabulous energy. Send out appreciation for the bounty of the earth and think about manifesting that bounty in whichever ways you need it most. Then say:

Gods of the harvest,

Abundant and overflowing,

Let that abundance come into my life

In whichever ways are best for me,

And grant me prosperity

In any and all positive forms.

So mote it be.

Deborah Blake

September 19
Sunday

2nd ♓

Color of the Day: Orange
Incense of the Day: Eucalyptus

Pine Cone Prosperity Spell

Here, we'll combine a classic fall craft with a little abundance magic. You'll need string, some pine cones, peanut butter, a spreading utensil of some kind, birdseed, and a plate.

Begin by tying a loop of string to the end of a pine cone—make it as long as you need to in order to hang your finished treat from an outdoor tree or plant hook! Next, use a butter knife or spoon to spread peanut butter generously on the pine cone. Be sure to get it into the crevices! Pour birdseed onto the plate, then roll the peanut butter–covered pinecone in the seed, coating it. As you roll, imagine your household full of warmth, health, and prosperity. Say:

By bird and cone and hearty seed,

We welcome friends come round to feed.

Of warmth and love in winter's chill,

May all who dwell here get their fill.

Hang your pine cones outside and enjoy watching the critters who snack on them!

Thorn Mooney

 ## September 20
Monday

2nd ♓

☽ v/c 7:55 pm

Full Moon 7:55 pm

☽ → ♈ 11:13 pm

Color of the Day: Silver
Incense of the Day: Clary sage

Sukkot begins at sundown

Full Moon in Pisces Tea Charm

The full moon today is in one of the most auspicious signs for magic, mysticism, and all things psychic—Pisces! It's the perfect time to perform acts of divination, to cross the hedge, to practice soul and astral body travel, and to listen to your instincts. Your magic today should reflect your internal needs at the moment, as Pisces makes us pay attention to such things. To help make those clear, here is a tea charm.

In a teacup, add one tablespoon of dried lavender, one whole small apple (cored and diced), a pinch of clove, and a tablespoon of honey. Fill with boiling water three-quarters of the way and let steep for five minutes. Before sipping, draw a pentacle over the cup in the air with your index finger and say:

Reveal to me the true desires within.

Devin Hunter

September 21
Tuesday

3rd ♈

Color of the Day: Maroon
Incense of the Day: Cedar

UN International Day of Peace

Eat an Apple

So many spells, incantations, and charms center around apples. Peel an apple in one long strip and toss it over your shoulder. The letter that the peel on the ground resembles is said to be the first letter of the name of your destined true love. This is a simplified version of a love spell found in numerous sources.

That is all well and good, but even better, eat an apple today. What an abundance there is from which to choose! Perhaps you already have a favorite, but if you have little experience with apples, explore the many possibilities. Consider a trip to your local farmers' market or orchards. Get on that hay wagon with a group of like-minded folks, pick to your heart's delight, and enjoy the fruits of your labors for days to come. In 2019 a new apple, the Cosmic Crisp, was introduced. Johnny Appleseed would be amazed!

Emyme

September 22
Wednesday

3rd ♈

☉ → ♎ 3:21 pm

☽ v/c 10:05 pm

Color of the Day: White
Incense of the Day: Lilac

Mabon – Fall Equinox

Put the Trees to Sleep

As a tree hugger, it seems logical to me to send trees love and peace at the end of their growing season. After all, they give us shade, oxygen, fruit, and more.

The Fall Equinox marks the day when the Wheel of the Year starts to turn toward the dark months. It's a perfect time to send some love and gratitude to ancient tree spirits, as soon they will lose their leaves and go dormant for the winter.

For this spell you will need 3 cups water in a pot and ½ cup each dried lavender, rose petals, and chamomile.

Bring the water to a boil on the stove, and add the herbs. Simmer for five minutes, then remove from the heat and let cool. Strain the mixture into a pitcher and go outdoors where your favorite trees live.

Pour a bit of the brew at the base of as many tree trunks as you like. Think about what they've provided over the summer, and feel gratitude for each one individually as you pour.

Tree spirits will be able to feel the appreciation in your offering and thoughts, which is a nice way to be put to bed for the winter.

Kate Freuler

Notes:

September 23
Thursday

3rd ♈

☽ → ♉ 8:38 am

Color of the Day: Green
Incense of the Day: Myrrh

Into the Dark Spell

N ow we enter the dark season. This is the time to get rid of any problems in your life—bad habits, relationships, jobs, etc. Perform this spell after dark. You'll need a silver ink pen or marker, a sheet of black construction paper, a heatproof container or cauldron, and a black candle.

First, write your problem on the paper. Read it aloud. Next, tear the paper into pieces and place them in the container/cauldron. Then safely light the candle. Now ignite the paper scraps with the candle flame as you say:

Hear me, season of the dark.

Consume my problems with this spark.

Paper, burn until you turn to ash.

Now I'm free of this problem at last!

When the ashes cool, throw them outside on the ground or in the trash. Extinguish the candle. When it's cool, throw it away.

James Kambos

September 24
Friday

3rd ♉

Color of the Day: Coral

Incense of the Day: Orchid

Roots of Nourishment

Though most meditative practices that focus on energetic roots are designed to ground and release, in nature the roots of a plant not only provide grounding and a strong foundation but also absorb vital nutrients and water from the earth. This spell calls upon the earth to exchange any incorrect or harmful energies that you may have, replacing them with new, healthy energy.

To begin, sit comfortably, close your eyes, and meditate. Begin to do a standard grounding by mentally sending etheric roots from your body into the ground. When you have reached this state, change your focus and then pull energy back up from the earth with the intention that this earth power will vitalize, nourish, and heal your mind, body, and spirit. Dwell in this state for as long as desired, then retract your roots and come out of the meditation.

Michael Furie

 ## September 25
Saturday

3rd ♉

☽ v/c 9:09 am

☽ → ♊ 8:36 pm

Color of the Day: Black

Incense of the Day: Magnolia

Altar Cleansing

It's a good idea to cleanse your altar on a regular basis to remove any lingering negative energy. Remove all the items and use a cleaner made from natural ingredients to remove dust and dirt. Then prepare this mixture for energy cleansing:

- 1 cup warm water
- 1 teaspoon lemon juice
- 1 sprig of fresh rosemary

Add the mixture to a spray bottle, shake well, and mist your altar as you chant the following:

Clean and clear,

Clean and clear,

Negativity disappear!

Wipe your altar dry and replace all the items—but make sure you clean those as well.

Ember Grant

September 26
Sunday

3rd ♊

Color of the Day: Gold
Incense of the Day: Heliotrope

Wind Power

As the seasons change and the strong winds blow, here is a spell to help you release the things that no longer serve you. On a windy day, utilize the force and power of this nature element. Go outside and stand in a spot where there is a strong wind. Stretch your arms out wide, close your eyes, and visualize in your mind's eye anything and everything that no longer serves your highest good falling away from you and disappearing into the wind. Say these words silently in your mind or out loud:

As the wind surrounds me, help me be free of all the things in my life that no longer serve me.

After you have said this chant, visualize yourself embracing this strong air element and welcome the winds of change.

Sapphire Moonbeam

September 27
Monday

3rd ♊

Color of the Day: Ivory
Incense of the Day: Rosemary

Sukkot ends

Pause and Give Thanks

Sukkot, the Jewish harvest festival, ends today. The sukkah, an outdoor reed hut, is where families eat, recalling the time when the Israelites wandered the desert for forty years, sleeping and eating under the stars.

Today, take time to get outside for a meal, and pause and give thanks for your harvest. Can you leave work at lunchtime to eat outdoors? Can you enjoy your evening meal on the deck or in the yard?

As you eat, slowly savor the food, being thankful for all that you eat.

Take time to appreciate where you live, work, or are, and give thanks for your home, workplace, and neighborhood.

Widen your awareness to the community, area, or town you are in, and give thanks for the safety, security, and services available to you.

When you finish your meal, pause and give thanks that you are housed, fed, protected, and cared for.

What a harvest!

Dallas Jennifer Cobb

September 28
Tuesday

3rd ♊

☽ v/c 12:18 am

☽ → ♋ 9:34 am

4th Quarter 9:57 pm

Color of the Day: White
Incense of the Day: Basil

Coconut Blessing

Lighting lamps and finding ways to battle back the shadow within us are common themes at this time of year. Ready your home for autumn gatherings by making coconut lanterns. Simply buy one or more coconuts and sit in a sacred space. Think of a prayer for a selfless and positive purpose. As you do so, pierce and drain the coconut using a hammer and a thick nail, drinking the juice to help fill you with the strength and courage to serve others this season.

Use the hammer to carefully split the coconut, then bake it in the oven at 300 degrees F. for one hour or until the meat pulls away from the shell. Grind or grate the fruit to make sweets and snacks or to enjoy over buttered popcorn. Place tealight candles, marigolds, and party charms or candies inside the shells, and leave these on the table or an altar to create a welcoming and warm home for the holiday season ahead.

Estha McNevin

September 29
Wednesday

4th ♋

Color of the Day: Yellow
Incense of the Day: Honeysuckle

Beans of Success

Today is National Coffee Day. Take time to celebrate this beverage of the gods. Coffee is an entheogen, opening connections to the divine. You may have heard it personified as the goddess Caffeina. It expands awareness, quickens thought, and hones focus. It also energizes the body. Coffee enables people to do many things that would be much harder without it. For this reason, it corresponds with success.

For this spell you will need a bag of coffee beans or ground coffee, whichever you prefer. (A plastic pod won't work, as plastic tends to insulate against magic.) Open the bag and smell the beans. Concentrate on how even the smell of coffee helps you wake up and focus. Then say:

Caffeina, goddess of coffee, bless these beans with the power of success. When I drink of your brew, may I become alert and capable.

Visualize the energy in the beans. Then seal the bag and brew a cup whenever you need to boost your success.

Elizabeth Barrette

September 30
Thursday

4th ♋

☽ v/c 10:49 am

☽ → ♌ 8:53 pm

Color of the Day: Crimson
Incense of the Day: Balsam

harvest Squash Bake

It's squash season! Zucchini and yellow squash are overflowing in grocery stores and farmers' markets. Here is a simple recipe to enjoy the abundance of squash season.

You will need:

- 3 yellow squash
- 3 zucchini
- 1 red bell pepper
- 1 tomato
- 1 tablespoon olive oil
- Seasonings of your choice (I like to use Italian seasoning, celery seed, pepper, and sea salt.)

Heat an oven to 350 degrees F.

While the oven is heating, slice all the vegetables. Place them in a bowl and add the olive oil and the seasonings. Arrange the vegetables in a glass baking dish. Bake for one hour.

For a complete meal, add a green salad and some crusty bread. Enjoy the abundance of the season and give thanks to Mother Earth for beautiful, bountiful squash!

Najah Lightfoot

Notes:

October

Days that turn on a breath into rapidly waning light. Wispy, high dark clouds in an orange and turquoise sky. Bright orange pumpkins carved into beautiful art and lit from inside. The eerie music of screeching cats. These fond images of October burn at a Witch's heart, calling to her even across the seasons where she's busy setting up her tent for festival. By the time October finally arrives, Witches and other magic users have already had discussions about costumes and parties, rituals and celebrations, and we look forward with happiness to the whole month of both poignantly somber and brightly playful activities.

In Celtic Europe, our ancestors acknowledged October as the last month of the summer season, with winter officially beginning on Samhain. They carved slits in squashes to keep light in the fields so they could finish their day's work, and when the custom came to America, it eventually evolved into the tradition of carving jack-o'-lanterns. American Witches often use magical symbols to carve their pumpkins, creating beacons for their Beloved Dead. In the spirit of the turn of energies at this time, we give candy to children to ensure that they, our future, will remember the sweetness inside and be good leaders when their turn comes. May we all be so blessed.

Thuri Calafia

October 1
Friday

4th ♌

Color of the Day: Pink
Incense of the Day: Mint

Attuning to Water

Now that we're past the autumn equinox, the shortening of the days is palpable. Even if your region doesn't see snow, the weather is likely cooler and rainier, and you may be noticing that the sun sets earlier, bringing lengthening periods of darkness. In many Western magical traditions, the autumn corresponds to the element of water, which is associated with mystery, depth, intuition, and feeling.

To make the most of the deepening, contemplative season, attune to the element of water. Sit in a cool bath or even a natural body of water, or simply place your hands in a full basin. Allow the water to move around you, filling every curve and crevice. Think about how the water moves and how it changes to reflect whatever contains it. Say:

*Powers of water, lend me your gifts
of compassion, intuition, and change.
Be with me this day. So mote it be.*

Thorn Mooney

October 2
Saturday

4th ♌
☽ v/c 7:43 pm

Color of the Day: Gray
Incense of the Day: Rue

Come Back to Me Spell

If you've misplaced something, this spell will help you find it. You'll need a plain sheet of white paper, a pen, and a pink piece of ribbon (or yarn) about three feet long.

Write the name of the lost item on the paper. You may also draw a picture of it. Roll the paper up and tie one end of the ribbon around the paper. Now sit at a table holding the loose end of the ribbon in your hand. The paper should be across the table from you. Ground and center. Softly say three times:

Come back to me.

Pull the paper toward you as you say this. Keep the ribbon attached to the paper, and lay the ribbon and paper on your altar. Don't think about it again. Later you'll get a feeling where the item is. You'll find it.

James Kambos

October 3
Sunday

4th ♌

☽ → ♍ 4:38 am

Color of the Day: Amber
Incense of the Day: Frankincense

Calling the Witch Ancestors

While modern jack-o'-lanterns are made from pumpkins, they were originally made from hollowed-out turnips. This spell honors the past and builds strength for the future. Gather these items:

- 1 turnip
- 1 black candle
- 1 mini pumpkin
- 1 white candle
- Incense (equal parts anise, coriander, and cardamom) and a censer

On a table, place the turnip to the left, with the black candle behind it. Place the pumpkin to the right, with the white candle behind it and the censer (unlit) between the candles. Think of the witches of the past who paved the way for our modern practice. Focus on asking them for guidance and help in advancing your craft. Safely light the black candle, then the white candle and incense, saying:

*To build a bond and call
on your power, hidden
company of witches past.*

*Grant me guidance and
strength this hour, I call those
before, this spell I cast.*

*For highest good, joyous and
free, as I will, so mote it be!*

Snuff out the candles and incense. Use the turnip and pumpkin as decorations to remind you of ancestor magic.

Michael Furie

NOTES:

October 4
Monday

4th ♏

Color of the Day: Gray
Incense of the Day: Narcissus

Rusty Nail Spell

The purpose of this amulet is to ward off unwanted visitors, such as nosy neighbors or people you just don't want in your home.

Gather these items:

- A rusted old nail (The dirtier and rustier it is, the better.)

- A piece of paper to wrap the nail in

- A pen

Hold the nail in your hand and think about how sharp and dangerous it is, and how much it would hurt if you stepped on it. While no one is going to actually physically step on the nail or get hurt, imagining this quality acknowledges its energy, which is defensive and best avoided.

Now imagine the person or people you want to keep out of your space. Write their name(s) on the paper, and wrap it around the nail.

Place the nail wrapped in the paper underneath the doormat to your home, with the point facing outward. Those who are unwanted will feel the energy of the rusty nail directed at them and hopefully take the hint.

Kate Freuler

October 5
Tuesday

4th ♏

☽ v/c 4:46 am
☽ → ♎ 8:41 am

Color of the Day: Scarlet
Incense of the Day: Cinnamon

Comfort and Joy

For me, there's a lot of comfort in a cup of tea. My childhood associations with tea are connected to memories of being safe, cared for, and loved. My British grandmother always made me tea and cookies, and I have many sweet associations.

Boil the kettle and make tea in a favorite mug. Wrap your hands around the mug and feel the comfort of the physical heat. Take a sip, and as the warm fluid slides down your throat, notice how content you feel with the warmth in your belly. With each sip, envision a caring person from your past beaming at you. Feel their love, support, and care. Drink in the comfort and joy.

Taking a few moments to slow down can lower blood pressure, reduce tension, and relax muscles. Using visualization, you can weave a magical blanket of comfort and joy to snuggle into, wrapping yourself in good feeling.

Dallas Jennifer Cobb

October 6
Wednesday

4th ♎

New Moon 7:05 am

Color of the Day: Brown
Incense of the Day: Bay laurel

The Silver Guide

For this spell you will need these items:

- A piece of silver (a coin, a piece of jewelry, a chain, etc.)
- Some dried lavender
- Some dried willow bark

Should you embark upon a quest,

In need of blessings and a guide,

On new moon's night
perform this spell,

And may the muses treat you well.

A piece of silver beneath
your pillow,

Along with lavender and willow.

Then speak these words
with eyes closed tight,

Before you go to sleep this night:

New moon, so dark, a promise yet,

Of light that grows in steady course.

Revealing paths as yet untrod,

I conjure forth the teaching dream.

Storm Faerywolf

October 7
Thursday

1st ♎

☽ v/c 1:03 am

☽ → ♏ 10:22 am

Color of the Day: White
Incense of the Day: Jasmine

Soil Spell for Abundance

For this spell you'll need a handful of soil, preferably from a garden where food crops have been growing all summer. If you can't obtain this, then some dirt from any place where plants are flourishing is fine. Cup the soil in your hands and meditate for a few moments on the significance of fertile land—how vital it is for all life on Earth. Speak these words:

Fecund land and fertile soil,
like the harvest that we reap.

Abundant Earth, please help me earn
prosperity that's mine to keep.

Visualize abundance filling your life in every way. Deposit the soil in your own yard or in a potted plant. If you took the soil from your own garden, then simply return it.

Ember Grant

October 8
Friday

1st ♏

Color of the Day: Coral
Incense of the Day: Violet

Love Apple

The apple has a long and sordid history of being a forbidden, seductive, and evil fruit. Let's bring the apple out of the darkness and embrace its good juju!

For this spell, cut a red apple in half, slicing horizontally. Remove the seeds and give one half of the apple to your lover. As the two of you eat your apples, say:

*As the fruit of the apple
falls from the tree,*

My love shall always remain with thee.

Plant the seeds in the earth.

If you're seeking to bring love into your life, carve the words "my true love" onto one half of the apple. Eat your half of the apple while lovingly holding the other half with the carved words in your hand. Bury the apple with the carved words in your back yard or in a flowerpot. That way, nature will help your love grow and blossom into something beautiful for you and your intended beloved.

Najah Lightfoot

October 9
Saturday

1st ♏

☽ v/c 2:05 am

☽ → ♐ 11:24 am

Color of the Day: Blue
Incense of the Day: Patchouli

Cast Iron Cauldron Crème

Applying crème to cast irons was a good Old World chore often done with prayers and a sense of wealth, because the fats used to temper cooking irons, even today, are among the most prized for baking. This highland crème is one that gives a shine and seals the outside of the pans, protecting them from soot and debris if they are used on a fire.

The season of the cauldron is a great time to practice traditional kitchen witchery and give thanks for how far we've come since the days when our every meal was cooked over an open fire. It works best to mix this crème by hand:

- 1 cup bacon lard or pork belly fat, rendered
- ½ cup beef fat
- ½ cup coconut fat, solid

Pack any remaining mixture in old toilet paper tubes, which can be stored in canning jars in the freezer when not in use. Enchant the mixture with your own spoken spells to the Great Goddess: the cauldron of life.

Estha McNevin

NOTES:

 October 10
Sunday

1st ♈ ♐

Color of the Day: Orange
Incense of the Day: Hyacinth

Firewood Spell

The fire element spreads its symbolic colors over the trees when their leaves change in autumn. It is an element we need more and more as the weather cools. Some people have a woodstove, a fireplace, or a firepit. For them, autumn is a time to cut and haul firewood or order a load to be delivered.

Here is a spell to keep your woodpile safe from pests or moisture and maximize the energy from it. You will need a stick of incense, preferably a woody scent such as pine, cedar, or sandalwood. You will also need a small piece of wood from your woodpile.

Safely light the incense and wave the wood through the smoke. Then say:

*Fire spirits, bless this wood. Keep
it safe from insects that nibble and
mice that gnaw. Keep it dry from
rain that dribbles and snow that
drifts. May it burn bright and hot
to warm my days once I light it.*

Then return the piece of wood to the woodpile.

Elizabeth Barrette

October 11
Monday

1st ♐

☽ v/c 12:30 am

☽ → ♑ 1:15 pm

Color of the Day: White
Incense of the Day: Hyssop

Columbus Day –
Indigenous Peoples' Day –
Thanksgiving Day (Canada)

Affirmation for Positive Change

Today is the day most Americans know as Columbus Day. It is also now called Indigenous Peoples' Day, in acknowledgment of the fact that there were indigenous people already living here when Columbus "discovered" the New World. It was, in fact, only new to him.

Our reality, or at least our awareness of it, is a constantly shifting and changing space. This can be tough to deal with, but it is important for us to constantly strive to change for the better. On this day in particular, and any other day that it feels right, try doing this simple affirmation or meditation. (You can do it as either or both.) Say:

I am open to positive change.
I work for positive change in
myself and in the world.

If you want, you can just sit with these words for a moment, or you can close your eyes and meditate on what a better world or a better self would look like to you.

Deborah Blake

NOTES:

October 12
Tuesday

1st ♑
2nd Quarter 11:25 pm

Color of the Day: Gray
Incense of the Day: Cedar

Elevate your Vibration with Music and Dance

Music and dancing are a great way to add joy and movement to enhance and raise power during magical workings. Since ancient times dance has been associated with spiritual events. The ancient Egyptians, as well as many other ancient societies, celebrated with music and dance in ceremonies to honor the gods and goddesses.

Add dance and rhythm to any of your spells with chants to help amplify the power. Say the words with the rhythm of the music of your choice or chant along with rattles or drumbeats that you create. Allow your body to move in sync and in harmony with the sounds. Dance uninhibitedly while you incorporate the rhythm and music into your movements. Don't overthink your dancing; get into the flow, enjoy yourself, and let yourself go.

Sapphire Moonbeam

October 13
Wednesday

2nd ♑
☽ v/c 6:53 am
☽ → ♒ 4:47 pm

Color of the Day: Topaz
Incense of the Day: Lavender

A Wishing Well Spell

On this day in ancient Rome, springs and wells were honored by casting floral garlands or wreaths into them. This spell helps us remember this ritual.

You'll need a bowl filled with spring water and two or three ivy leaves. Sit before the bowl of water. Drop the ivy leaves into the water. Dip a finger into the water and anoint your third eye. Now close your eyes and meditate about a wish you want to come true. Open your eyes and stir the water clockwise three times with your finger. Carry the bowl outside and place the ivy leaves on the ground as an offering. Then pour the water on a tree or shrub, or water a houseplant with it. Your wish will manifest itself soon.

James Kambos

October 14
Thursday

2nd ≈

Color of the Day: Purple
Incense of the Day: Mulberry

Drown Out the Buzz of Lack

We live in the happy knowledge that abundance is ours. There is enough and more of everything we truly need. Believing in it makes it so.

Unfortunately, there are people who are just as convinced of, and living in, lack. Believing in that also makes it so. It may be possible to nudge some of these folks from pessimism to optimism. But for those stuck in an eternal downward spiral, it might be best to leave them alone. Take yourself out of their sphere. Put in your earbuds and enjoy some soothing music. When those options are not viable, learn to drown out the buzz. Concentrate on all things good and happy. This isn't always an easy skill to develop, but it will save you headaches, both literal and figurative. Call upon Tranquillitas, goddess of peace and tranquility. She will guide you to serenity in the face of discontent. Say:

Quiet the noise, block the whine,
create a wall of calm divine. Offer a
smile, perhaps a soft word. Abundance
is forever and lack deterred.

Emyme

 October 15
Friday

2nd ≈

☽ v/c 8:33 am
☽ → ♓ 10:22 pm

Color of the Day: Rose
Incense of the Day: Alder

Rise Above It Spell

Both the sun and Mars are in Libra today, bringing about a strong desire for people to find middle ground and transcend issues. It is a time when the cosmos is calling us to let go of our ego. Sometimes this is hard, but don't worry—this spell is meant to help you take the high road when it would be easier to take a lower one or not budge at all.

In a medium-size bowl, put one cup of salt, three sprigs of fresh peppermint, the peel of one whole lemon, and three pinches of catnip. Using your index finger, stir the ingredients together and visualize the problem moving from your mind down into the bowl through your finger, and allow the mixture to absorb it. Lift the bowl over your head and walk counterclockwise in a small circle three times. As you do this, say:

I rise above this mess that's made,
and now I see resistance fade.

Put the bowl in a western corner and leave it there until the matter is resolved.

Devin Hunter

October 16
Saturday

2nd ♓

Color of the Day: Gray
Incense of the Day: Pine

Apple Peel Divination

This time of year is wonderful for divining the future! Try this variation on an American colonial classic, derived from Dutch folklore.

In colonial New England, young girls would peel an apple in one continuous strand, then throw the peel over their shoulder to reveal the initial of their future husband. If you happen to be in the market for a husband, then by all means give it a try!

But this technique can be used to divine other information as well: to reveal other names, significant numbers, or meaningful shapes. Begin by asking the apple a question. Use a sharp knife to peel it in one long piece while concentrating on your request, then toss it over your shoulder to reveal an answer! A peel that lands in a heart or star shape might indicate coming love or excitement. A *Y* or *N* could be *yes* or *no*. A letter might give a clue to someone who will influence you. Keep an open mind and follow your intuition!

Thorn Mooney

 October 17
Sunday

2nd ♓
☽ v/c 7:24 pm

Color of the Day: Yellow
Incense of the Day: Marigold

Cleansing a Pre-owned Object

I love thrift stores, antique shops, flea markets, etc. My partner and I have a collection of chalices, many books, and even a brass cauldron and statuettes of the Venus de Milo and Isis that have been gathered over the years from local shops. The only drawback is that you cannot be certain of the history of pre-owned items, so it's a good idea to cleanse them in order to neutralize any energetic residue they may contain.

First, physically clean the object in whichever way is proper, then proceed with the cleansing. Two quick and effective options for this are to pass the object through the smoke of frankincense and myrrh incense, or touch the object with both hands and visualize all the energy in the object changing from cloudy to clear, and say:

A safe addition to my domain,
cleared and cleansed you will be.

No harmful power shall you contain,
filled only with correct, healthy energy.
Michael Furie

October 18
Monday

2nd ♓

☽ → ♈ 6:04 am

Color of the Day: Ivory
Incense of the Day: Neroli

An Act for Humanity

The number eighteen in numerology is often said to vibrate with the concept of humanitarianism. Most people on a magical path are deeply devoted to nature. In reality, devotion to nature is truly of humanitarian benefit. If we do not maintain the integrity of the natural ecosystems and life forms we are interdependent on, we will drive ourselves to eventual extinction.

Today, make an effort to contribute in some way, even if small, through an act of humanitarian benefit. Perhaps that is directly, by donating food, money, or time to a homeless shelter or charity, or perhaps it is through an environmental effort, such as helping pollinators or birds by hanging feeders or pollinator houses. Journal about what you choose to do and how you can contribute to humanitarian efforts in the future on a regular basis. Small efforts can add up to big results, especially when we all do our part. So mote it be.

Blake Octavian Blair

 October 19
Tuesday

2nd ♈

Color of the Day: Red
Incense of the Day: Ginger

Lollipop Divination

Nothing says October like candy! Get yourself a bag of multicolored lollipops, making sure they're all individually packaged. Shake the bag to mix them up while asking this question:

What do I need to focus on in my life this week?

Close your eyes and pull a lollipop out of the bag. Your answer lies in the color:

• *Red:* Focus on your romantic life.

• *Pink:* You need to pay attention to nurturing friendships.

• *Orange:* Hone in on your passions and hobbies.

• *Yellow:* Take time to make sure you and others are feeling positive in general.

• *Green:* Pay attention to your finances.

• *Blue:* Communication between you and the people in your life is extra important right now.

- *Purple:* Make sure you spend time on your spiritual practice and meditation.
- *Black:* Be sure to guard yourself energetically against others.
- *White:* Spirit has an important message or lesson for you this week, so pay attention.

Now the best part: enjoy the candy!

Kate Freuler

NOTES:

October 20
Wednesday

2nd ♈

☽ v/c 10:57 am

Full Moon 10:57 am

☽ → ♉ 3:59 pm

Color of the Day: White
Incense of the Day: Marjoram

Charging Spell

On this full moon, charge some of your magical objects (tools, crystals, etc.) in the moonlight. Even if it's cloudy, that's okay. Place your objects outside in a protected place or inside on a windowsill. Visualize the moonlight charging the items with potent magical energy. Chant these words before leaving your items in place for the night:

> Moonlight, cast your magic glow
> upon these items that I choose.
>
> Moonlight, with your energy
> these items now infuse.

Ember Grant

October 21
Thursday

3rd ♉

Color of the Day: Crimson
Incense of the Day: Myrrh

Receive the Blessing of an Ancestral Spirit

For this spell you will need these materials:

- White cord, chalk, salt, or other objects to mark out a circle on the floor
- A white and a black candle
- A vase with fresh flowers
- A piece of paper with the name of an ancestor written upon it
- A cauldron or ash pot

When you would ask a spirit dear,
To bring forth blessings
and draw them near,
Just mark a circle on the ground,
With cord or chalk or
whatever's found.
Just be it white like shining moon,
Then light a candle black as doom.
Present here now a vase of flowers,
An offering unto ancient powers.

And speak aloud these
words of rhyme,
To seal thy charm and
make it thine:

Spirit come with love and grace,
All else denied this hallowed space.

From the deep black candle's flame,
Now light the white and
speak the name
Of someone whom
you've lost from life,
To bring you blessings
and ease all strife.
Burn the paper from the white,
And cast it to the cauldron now,
And speak here to your
spirit bright,
To end when candles
do burn down.

Storm Faerywolf

October 22
Friday

3rd ♉

☽ v/c 4:35 pm

Color of the Day: Pink
Incense of the Day: Rose

Wiccan Spell Jars

For many Wiccans and Pagans, getting to know our culture and sharing it with others has become a fun way to celebrate October. It's fun to see witchy movies on every channel, including the ol' pointy hats and golden buckles like it's 1746! Take it up a notch today by picking three facts about witchcraft that matter to you and sharing them with people you know and love.

Gather three spell jars (about 7 by 2 inches each). Inside each jar, place a cinnamon stick, a pinch of dried witch hazel herb, and a small charm stone (or other spiritual object). Include an image and a fact about witchcraft that is easily readable through the jar. (Print out an image and write a fact upon it.) Place the jars on a family altar, holiday table, or windowsill to promote gratitude and knowledge of our culture this season.

Estha McNevin

 ## October 23
Saturday

3rd ♉

☉ → ♏ 12:51 am

☽ → ♊ 3:57 am

Color of the Day: Black
Incense of the Day: Ivy

Moving Divination

Autumn is a time when the crops are harvested and then the fields lie fallow. Everything that works needs a rest sometimes, so now is a good time to consider which parts of your life could use a break. This is especially important if you feel overloaded with too much to do.

For this moving divination, make a list of significant parts of your life that take up your time and energy. Five to ten is a good range. Hold those in your mind as you take a walk. Ideally walk around your neighborhood, school, or workplace—someplace you know well. If you see something that reminds you of a point on your list, take note that this is an area of your life that needs some rest. Try to schedule downtime for it, or at least avoid adding new projects. In spring, you can renew the activity again.

Elizabeth Barrette

October 24
Sunday

3rd ♊

Color of the Day: Gold
Incense of the Day: Eucalyptus

Lucky Penny Prosperity Spell

Financial stability is largely the result of a combination of good habits, discipline, and know-how, but sometimes we just need a helping hand or a bit of luck. That luck often comes from unexpected places, like when we find a dropped coin on the sidewalk or a dollar bill pressed into the pages of a used book.

To draw money into your household, begin collecting the lucky pennies (and other coins) you find during your day-to-day life and keep them at the threshold of your home. You might line them up on the molding of the front door or place them in a potted plant outside—whatever is most appealing to you. Every time you find a new coin, place it with the others and say:

Money finds its way to me.

Wealth and luck flow naturally.

Trust that prosperity will be drawn to you and won't leave your home easily.

Thorn Mooney

October 25
Monday

3rd ♊

☽ v/c 10:11 am

☽ → ♋ 5:00 pm

Color of the Day: Silver
Incense of the Day: Rosemary

Fall Cleaning

Most people do spring cleaning, but you might consider adding some magical fall cleaning to your routine as well. After all, in many parts of the country, cold weather means you're stuck in your home a lot more, with few or no chances to open the windows and refresh the energy. So it's a good idea to go into the season with as clear and clean a space as possible.

This means practical cleaning too, of course, but you may want to add a magical element as well. You can create some magical cleaning water by adding any essential oil that is good for cleansing (like orange or lemon) and then blessing it before you use it. Then dip a broom into the water and go from room to room with the intention of clearing away any negative or stagnant energy. If you can, open the windows and waft it right out!

Deborah Blake

October 26
Tuesday

3rd ♋

Color of the Day: Gray
Incense of the Day: Geranium

Prayers for Prosperity

The law of attraction holds that what we give thanks for is magnetized to us, and what we focus on grows. Today, let us give thanks for money and grow our prosperity. Each time you reach into your wallet, say:

Thank you for all the money I have.

When you pay for something, say:

I am grateful for all the resources I enjoy.

When someone gives you change, say:

I am thankful for all the money that has been given to me.

If you find money or a treasure or stone, say:

I welcome all the abundance that flows to me.

Whatever the transaction is, let your prayers for prosperity be heard. Speak them out loud so others hear your gratitude. Build the magnetic resonance of gratitude, and let it grow strong. Know that by giving thanks and saying prayers for prosperity, you will attract more money and prosperity to you.

Dallas Jennifer Cobb

October 27
Wednesday

3rd ♋

Color of the Day: Yellow
Incense of the Day: Lilac

Feast the Dead Spell

The spirit world is close to us in October. This is a good time to let the spirit realm know we're thinking of them. One of the best ways to do this is to "feed" the spirits.

For this ritual you'll need a red apple. Apples are traditionally one of the main foods used to honor the deceased. Perform this ritual tonight if it's windy or on any other windy autumn night. First, wash the apple and wipe it dry. Then hold the apple and say:

Tonight as the wild winds roar,

I set this apple by my door.

This ancient fruit so red,

Help me honor and feast the dead.

Abroad in the night or beyond the stars,

I honor all spirits wherever they are.

Now place the apple outside by your door. In the morning, if the apple is still there, place it gently in a wooded area or bury it. The spirits will thank you in positive ways.

James Kambos

October 28
Thursday

3rd ♋

☽ v/c 2:02 am

☽ → ♌ 5:07 am

4th Quarter 4:05 pm

Color of the Day: Green
Incense of the Day: Clove

The Mighty Chestnut

They're chartreuse-colored and spiky. They look like something from a children's storybook. Folk magick manuals say they're used in love and prosperity spells. Grown-ups have childhood memories of drilling holes in them and playing games with them, and squirrels devour and bury them with glee. At Yule and Christmastime, a favorite song about roasting them over an open fire plays over and over again. The mighty chestnut, how we adore thee!

For this spell you will need three chestnuts. Hold them in your hands and say:

Mighty chestnut, three times three,

From spiky green to magnificent tree.

Powers of love and prosperity,

Thank you for granting these to me!

Place the chestnuts on your prosperity altar or bury them in your back yard.

Najah Lightfoot

October 29
Friday

4th ♌

Color of the Day: Purple
Incense of the Day: Vanilla

Hermit Day Meditation

October 29 is known as National Hermit Day. The Hermit card in the tarot refers to the need to experience solitude in an effort to do some soul-searching and gain spiritual insight from the silence. Time spent alone is important in order to become more grounded and centered and begin anew on your spiritual path. Practicing meditation will help you access the whispers of your soul and connect you to the voice of your spirit guides and the divine.

Sit in a comfortable position or lie on the floor. Take several deep cleansing breaths with your eyes closed and dive into the depths of your third eye. Do not try to control or anticipate what you might see. Breathe deeply and evenly until you are in the flow, and relax while you discover where your meditative visions take you.

Sapphire Moonbeam

October 30
Saturday

4th ♌

☽ v/c 3:05 am

☽ → ♍ 2:09 pm

Color of the Day: Blue
Incense of the Day: Sandalwood

Decaying Leaf Spell

The sun is already in Scorpio and Mars enters Scorpio today, so we can officially say that Samhain season is in full swing! Scorpio has a connection to death and decay, so now is the perfect time to tap into these influences for our magic. Cast this spell to watch a problem disappear.

Take a freshly fallen leaf and, with black marker, write the name of something that you wish to leave your life. Take this leaf away from your property—a graveyard would be best—and release it into a pile of other leaves. As you do this, say:

As you rot, so too will my problem.

Immediately turn your back on it and walk away.

Devin Hunter

 October 31
Sunday

4th ♍

Color of the Day: Orange
Incense of the Day: Heliotrope

Samhain – Halloween

Connect with the Ancestors

Samhain has arrived! Honoring and connecting with the ancestors is traditional on this day. Although we all have many types of ancestors, most of them fall in one or more of these three categories: ancestors of blood, ancestors of spirit (or tradition), and ancestors of the land.

Gather three candles, one each for the ancestors of blood, spirit, and land. Set them up in safe holders on your altar, and decorate the altar with any ancestor-related items you wish. Feel free to place offerings such as fresh flowers or a glass of water on the altar for your beloved ancestors. When you are ready to begin, ring a bell or chime and light the candles one by one, pausing after you light each candle to meditate on and pray to the ancestors it represents. When finished, ring the bell once more and allow the candles to safely burn out in their holders.

Blake Octavian Blair

November

The sounds of nature begin to quiet down in November, but this month is far from silent. Yes, the cheery morning birdsong of spring is gone, and crickets are no longer fiddling on warm summer afternoons, but November has its own "voices." On a frosty November morning, you'll hear a faint, faraway gabble. Raise your eyes toward the sky, and coming over the horizon, in a V formation heading south, is a flock of wild geese. The sound makes you pause and wonder: how do they know it's time to migrate? As you rake leaves, the late autumn breeze stirs them, and they softly rustle as they click and swirl up the street. Few sounds say November like the wind. It may be as gentle as a baby's breath or it may roar, carrying the weight of the coming winter as it howls in the night. During the night you can also hear November's most haunting voice: the lone hooting of an owl. Yes, this month has many voices, but every evening I hear the most comforting voice of all. That voice belongs to the crackling of burning logs as my hearth fire wards off the chill of a dark November night.

During this mysterious month, let the voices of November speak to you, igniting your imagination and your magic.

James Kambos

November 1
Monday

4th ♏

☽ v/c 1:00 pm

☽ → ♎ 7:11 pm

Color of the Day: Lavender
Incense of the Day: Lily

All Saints' Day

Amulet of Protection

Today is All Saints' Day. Historically, this was a time to honor obscure saints who might otherwise be forgotten. People would also honor their personal saints. Afro-Caribbean traditions connect Christian saints with African loas or orishas. Some Pagans observe this as a holiday for all deities, especially the minor ones who can get overlooked.

That is an ideal time for broad-spectrum protection spells. Get an amulet that depicts several deities or traditions that you like. Many interfaith buttons or pendants can serve this purpose. Cleanse the amulet with salt and water, and bless it with a sacred incense such as frankincense, myrrh, cedar, sage, or eucalyptus. If you have favorite saints, orishas, or other patrons, then name them.

Finally, say:

All little gods and minor goddesses,
hidden spirits of all kinds, I honor
you today and ask for your protection.
Keep me safe from all harm.

Carry the amulet with you for safety.

Elizabeth Barrette

NOTES:

November 2
Tuesday

4th ♎︎

Color of the Day: Scarlet
Incense of the Day: Ylang-ylang

Election Day (general)

Inner Vision

When this spell was written, it was the year 2019. At that time, we had no idea who would be elected the forty-sixth president of the United States. As you read these words now in the year 2021, a new president is in office and the presidential election of 2020 is a memory.

Magick is about believing and having faith in our ability to effect positive change. Maybe you voted, maybe you didn't. Maybe you're an activist or fed up entirely with the election process.

Wherever you may be today, be grateful for the rights we have, the civil rights many continue to fight for, and our ability to practice magick that can help ourselves, our loved ones, and the causes near and dear to our hearts. Blessed be.

Najah Lightfoot

November 3
Wednesday

4th ♎︎

☽ v/c 6:32 pm
☽ → ♏︎ 8:52 pm

Color of the Day: Topaz
Incense of the Day: Honeysuckle

Sisters' Plait Prayer

The season of family and holiday gatherings can fill us with a sense of dread if we don't have common tasks at hand to keep us busy and focused on the real reasons we have to celebrate. Braiding and brushing hair is something that targets our core instincts of social comfort and familiarity. When we let someone close to our hair, we are trusting that they will make us look and feel good about ourselves.

We can also choose to learn new braids and innovative ways to help others look their best. Take some time today to braid a friend's or sister's hair, visit the salon, or otherwise treat yourself to that feeling of comfort and security. As you get your hair done or do someone else's, say or think the flowing prayer:

Sisters, we work together effortlessly,

Woven in trinity.

Stronger together,

We share our energy.

Estha McNevin

November 4
Thursday

4th ♏

New Moon 5:15 pm

Color of the Day: Turquoise
Incense of the Day: Balsam

A Creative Push

From time to time, we all get bogged down in our jobs, hobbies, or spellwork. For an extra creative push, safely light a candle. For this time of year, as we move away from Samhain and toward Yule, choose a candle with an aroma that is a combination of orange spicy and red peppermint.

There are times when candles are not an option. One solution is heated plug-ins, which offer just as many seasonal scents. Yet even they can be a problem in places where no flame or heat is allowed. In that case, scented beads are the perfect solution. These, too, come in diverse scents appropriate for any season or occasion. All of these options can be found in supermarkets and specialty stores.

As you light your candle, say:

*At those times when my light burns
low, an extra push will follow.*

*With soft flame and warm scents,
watch the creativity flow.*

Be sure to extinguish the flame.

Emyme

 November 5
Friday

1st ♏

☽ v/c 12:10 pm

☽ → ♐ 8:52 pm

Color of the Day: White
Incense of the Day: Cypress

Flower Blessing

The secret language of flowers teaches that each kind of flower holds a symbolic meaning, as does each color. Buy potted or cut flowers and bring energy and blessings into your home. Doing small sacred acts to raise both your energy and that of your house and hearth can counteract the low feeling brought on by the decrease in sunlight hours at this time of year.

Carnations symbolize divine love. The white ones connote innocence and purity; the pink, admiration and respect; and the red, love and heartfelt desire. Roses symbolize earthly love, with rosebuds representing childhood and youth and the full flowers representing adulthood. White roses are symbolic of innocent or secret love, light pink of joy and blessings, rich pink of gratitude and appreciation, and red of romantic love and commitment, and a dark crimson symbolizes the mourning of lost love.

Choose the loving message you most need now, and bless your home and life with flowers.

Dallas Jennifer Cobb

November 6
Saturday

1st ♐

Color of the Day: Brown
Incense of the Day: Magnolia

Simple Meditation Amulet

Meditation is something that we all can benefit from, but it doesn't necessarily come easy to everyone. I know I struggled to get the hang of it and still find myself hitting the occasional block. I created this simple meditation amulet to help me deepen my skills with each session.

To create your own meditation amulet, you will need a small magnifying glass, a black marker, and a thick piece of cord or string to make a strap so you can wear it over your neck.

On the magnifying glass, draw a large eye with the marker. In the center of the eye, draw a pentacle. Look through the center of the pentacle and say:

Deep within the mysteries hide;

Find the patience that's locked inside.

Help me go deeper than I know I've been,

To explore the secrets of now and then.

Tie the ends of the cord around the handle of the magnifying glass, and wear your amulet during meditation.

Devin Hunter

November 7
Sunday

1st ♐

☽ v/c 8:44 am

☽ → ♑ 8:03 pm

Color of the Day: Gold
Incense of the Day: Hyacinth

Daylight Saving Time
ends at 2:00 a.m.

Coin Toss Spell

When you are searching for an answer to a yes-no question, you can use a coin to get results. Make sure you really want to know the answer before you begin. Depending on the situation, sometimes it may be better not to know.

Once you have decided to explore this simple form of divination, designate one side of the coin for a "yes" answer and the other side for a "no." First you must establish a relationship with the coin. Start by asking simple questions. Ask the coin if you are wearing shoes, for instance. Once the coin has provided you with three correct answers in a row, you may proceed and ask the question that you are most curious about. Take a deep breath and ask for an answer to your question. Flip the coin to see the result. Trust the answer you receive.

Sapphire Moonbeam

November 8
Monday

1st ♑

Color of the Day: Ivory
Incense of the Day: Narcissus

house Blessing

Your home—whether it is a house, an apartment, or even just a room—is where your heart is. It is the center of your existence, and it is important that you feel safe and secure when you are in it. Once a year, or more often if you live someplace that feels vulnerable, it is a good idea to do a house blessing. This is a nice way to reinforce any protection work you might have done and to ask for the gods to watch over you.

Light a sage smudge stick and hold it in front of you. First turn to the east, then the south, west, and north, asking each associated element (air, fire, water, and earth) to bless and protect your home. Then hold up the smudge stick and ask the God and Goddess to bless and protect your home. If you like, walk through each room with the smudge stick before putting it out safely. Watch out for stray sparks and stamp them out if you see them.

Deborah Blake

November 9
Tuesday

1st ♑

☽ v/c 12:51 pm

☽ → ♒ 10:03 pm

Color of the Day: Maroon
Incense of the Day: Bayberry

Supercharged Water Scrying

Scrying is the art of divination by gazing usually into a dark surface such as a black mirror or pool of water or ink, but there is also the classic crystal gazing. This method is cauldron scrying but with the added empowerment of an herbal brew that magically charges the water with visionary qualities and readies the psychic mind to properly receive and interpret the impressions given.

Gather the following:

• ¼ cup mugwort

• ¼ cup wormwood

• 2 cups water

If you wish, the brew can be made in a regular pot and then poured into your cauldron so you won't have to wait for the cauldron to cool before working. In any case, simmer the herbs in the water over low heat for about ten to fifteen minutes, then remove from the heat and strain the brew. Move to your working area and gaze into the liquid. Note any visions or impressions received.

Michael Furie

November 10
Wednesday

1st ≈

Color of the Day: White
Incense of the Day: Bay laurel

Procrastinator's Spell

For focus and motivation, obtain these three stones: yellow fluorite to promote creativity, citrine quartz for intellectual stimulation, and carnelian for motivation. Use this chant to charge the stones with your intent:

Give me the push I need to proceed,

To move forward, be inspired,
get things done, and succeed,

To meet all my deadlines
and be on time,

To help me make progress
and not fall behind.

State your intent. Carry the stones with you or keep them in your work area.

Ember Grant

November 11
Thursday

1st ≈

2nd Quarter 7:46 am

☽ v/c 2:52 pm

Color of the Day: Purple
Incense of the Day: Apricot

Veterans Day –
Remembrance Day (Canada)

Lay Down Your Arms

Today is Veterans Day, and for many Americans this is when we honor those who have served in the armed forces. Elsewhere in the world, today marks Armistice Day and Remembrance Day, during which we celebrate the end of World War I.

In honor of this, today is an ideal day to bring an end to a personal battle you may be fighting. Are you harboring a grudge or dwelling on a lost fight? War is sometimes necessary and just, but many of us at times find ourselves engaged in conflicts that are purely destructive.

To relieve yourself of a personal conflict that is holding you back, write your grievance on a piece of rice paper and hold a funeral for it off your property. Dig a grave and lay your grudge to rest. Eulogize your loss and lay flowers, then cover the grave with dirt. Turn around to leave and do not look back!

Thorn Mooney

November 12
Friday

2nd ≈

☽ → ♓ 2:54 am

Color of the Day: Rose
Incense of the Day: Thyme

Everyday Superpowers

Today is the anniversary of comic book writer Stan Lee's death in 2018. Lee's fantastic tales of superheroes remind us that even if we don't have such dramatic powers, we can be superheroes in our everyday lives.

What do you do in the world to help others? Do you use your gifts to benefit the world? Light a candle and engage the fire element in the form of passion. Journal about what your passions are, and brainstorm ways you can use them to do good in the world. Perhaps you help an elderly neighbor or you tutor students who need help after school. Maybe you have a talent such as art or music, and you offer lessons to those who lack opportunity. Whatever your strengths are, employ those as your superpowers to make the world a better place! Be sure to extinguish the candle when you're done.

Blake Octavian Blair

November 13
Saturday

2nd ♓

Color of the Day: Blue
Incense of the Day: Sandalwood

An Inner Journey Spell

November is a good time to journey inside ourselves to find the answers we seek. For this spell you'll need a white cloth, a white votive candle, and the Hermit card from a tarot deck.

Cover your altar with the cloth and light the candle. Then lay the Hermit card in front of the candle. Study the card. The Hermit is your guide for this inner journey. He's all-knowing. He wants to help, but you must listen—to your inner voice. Concentrate on your question and say:

*Hermit, guide me along
the path I should go.*

*Reveal to me the wisdom
I should know.*

Meditate on your need for no more than ten minutes, then thank the Hermit and go about your daily routine. Leave the card on your altar for about a day, then return the card to its deck. The answer will come to you. Use the cloth and candle for other meditations.

James Kambos

♡ November 14
Sunday

2nd ♓

☽ v/c 12:40 am

☽ → ♈ 10:48 am

Color of the Day: Yellow
Incense of the Day: Almond

Gifts from the heart

With only forty more days until Christmas Eve, we are approaching peak holiday shopping season. This year, consider giving earth-based holiday gifts. For family and friends who travel the same spiritual path, gift them with ingredients and spells packed in decorated tins, bottles, and jars. For those who follow a different path, gift them with ingredients for baking or cooking, along with recipes, all packed in festive reusable containers. Let your creativity flow!

If you have always created your own gifts, try a new craft. Or if you have never given homemade gifts, there is still time to sign up for a class on woodcrafts, ceramics, mosaics, candles, or soaps. As you create and assemble your presents, add some magic to them with this verse:

This gift is made with magic and love, from my hands and heart to your hands and heart.

Emyme

✈ November 15
Monday

2nd ♈

Color of the Day: Silver
Incense of the Day: Neroli

Sweet Words Spell

Venus is in Capricorn today, bringing our relationships and matters of the home front and center. We might just find ourselves getting into arguments with our partners or close friends and family. Add the holiday tension many of us are feeling to the mix and, well, things could get rough! Cast this spell to have what you say be heard and to have your opinion be desired rather than dismissed.

To do this spell, all you need is some honey. About a teaspoon will do just fine. If you do not have honey, feel free to use any type of sweet syrup. Place the honey on your tongue, but do not swallow. Instead, close your eyes and swirl it around in your mouth. When your mouth is sufficiently coated, say:

As this honey is sweet to me,

So shall my words to you be!

Then swallow and speak your words with confidence for all to hear.

Devin hunter

November 16
Tuesday

2nd ♈

☽ v/c 10:51 am

☽ → ♉ 9:18 pm

Color of the Day: Black
Incense of the Day: Cedar

Rose Milk

Roses are famous for their association with love of all kinds—romance, friendship, goodwill, devotion, and more. Something many people don't realize is that rose petals are also edible. To make rose milk, you will need one fresh rose and a cup of milk (either dairy or vegan). Make absolutely certain your rose comes from an organic source and has not been sprayed with chemicals.

Pull the petals off the rose one by one and place them in the shape of a heart on your altar or any flat surface. Put the glass of milk in the center. Visualize pink, loving light all around the rose petals. Now drop the petals into the milk one at a time. With each petal, state out loud something you'd like to attract in a relationship, such as trust, affection, support, or physical chemistry.

Allow the petals to sit in the milk for an hour in the fridge, then strain them out and dispose of them. Drink the milk or add it to your cereal or coffee. Focus on the pink vibrations that are now in your body, drawing loving energies straight to you.

Kate Freuler

NOTES:

November 17
Wednesday

2nd ♉

Color of the Day: Brown
Incense of the Day: Lilac

All My Luggage Spell

Many people travel at this time of year. Though it's nice to have the freedom to travel, the hassles can be frustrating, one of the worst being lost luggage. Even if you don't have immediate travel plans, this spell can prepare you for when you do.

You will need your suitcase(s) or other travel bag(s), a spool of wide, brightly colored ribbon, and scissors.

Ground and center. Measure and cut a length of ribbon, roughly nine feet long, for each of your bags, plus a shorter one about six feet. Tie each longer ribbon to a bag, saying:

Ribbon bright, I tie you here,

To keep my luggage safe and near.

The final ribbon you will carry with you while you travel, as a link to the others. Tie a knot in it and say:

A final knot to keep the others

Bound to me by silken colors.

Travel well!

Storm Faerywolf

 November 18
Thursday

2nd ♉

Color of the Day: Green
Incense of the Day: Jasmine

Dream Pillow Healing

The root of health is sleep. The best healing happens at night. If you can't sleep well, you probably don't heal well either. So focus on ensuring a good night's sleep to improve the rest of your health.

You can make a dream pillow by sewing a pouch or by putting one drawstring bag inside another, with their cinched openings in opposite directions. Fill the pouch with herbs for healing and sleep. A good combination of seven magical herbs is hops, chamomile, catnip, lavender, mint, rose petals, and sage. Use organic herbs if you can find and afford them. Fill most of the space with hops and/or chamomile, then add smaller amounts of the other herbs. Close the pouch by sewing it shut or pulling the drawstrings. Then say:

Sweet herbs, send me peaceful
sleep and heal me in the night.

Tuck the dream pillow into your bed and sleep with it at night.

Elizabeth Barrette

November 19
Friday

2nd ♉

☽ v/c 3:57 am

☽ Full Moon 3:57 am

☽ → ♊ 9:33 am

Color of the Day: Coral
Incense of the Day: Yarrow

Lunar Eclipse

Strengthen Your Foundation

Early today, the sun is in Scorpio and the moon is in the opposing sign of Taurus. These are both "fixed" signs that prefer a strong foundation and a steady environment. Their near-perfect opposition today, with the earth caught in the middle (the eclipse), can result in a chaotic vibe. We can use magic to transform this condition. You'll need a small table, a white candle, a black candle, and a chair.

Place the black candle on the left side of the table and the white one on the right. Safely light the candles, first the left one and then the right. Sit in the chair, placing both feet flat on the floor and both hands flat on the table, one in front of each candle. Close your eyes and feel yourself magnetically held in place. Feel solid and strong, fixed in place to the earth, where nothing can disturb you. Say this verse three times:

Chaos return to calm, foundation steady and strong.

Open your eyes and extinguish the candles.

Michael Furie

NOTES:

November 20
Saturday

3rd ♊

Color of the Day: Gray
Incense of the Day: Pine

Fuzzy Slipper Magick

Today we're going to use our third eye vision and look ahead into the future. I'm envisioning a day in the near future when you'll want to relax, let go, and *be*. It will come after a time when you've been working hard spiritually, emotionally, or physically. This will be the day when you'll need some fuzzy slipper magick.

Today, cast your eyes into the future and visualize a special pair of slippers or socks that make you feel instantly relaxed and comforted. Hold to that vision and visit it frequently until you see those magickal socks or slippers appear in an ad or a store. On that day, purchase or procure those slippers so that when your day of need arises, you will have magickally brought into being that which you need most, solidifying your power to visualize and manifest.

Najah Lightfoot

 ## November 21
Sunday

3rd ♊

☽ v/c 10:52 am

☉ → ♐ 9:34 pm

☽ → ♋ 10:33 pm

Color of the Day: Amber
Incense of the Day: Juniper

Solar Energy and Inspiration

The sun is great to work with for a burst of motivating energy and forward movement. A simple tool that represents all these energies in one concise focal point is the Sun card in the major arcana of the tarot. For today, put the Sun from your favorite tarot deck on your altar, and gather a carnelian or citrine stone and a white or yellow candle. Arrange the items on your altar, and light the candle, placed in a holder in which it can safely burn down. Bring your attention to a task that you've lacked motivation to do. Focus on the tarot image, and see the radiant light of the Sun imbuing you with energy. Feel yourself beginning to glow with warm, radiant, glowing energy. Feel the inspiration welling up within you, and pay attention as ideas come to mind of how you can spring into action on your task.

Blake Octavian Blair

November 22
Monday

3rd ♋

Color of the Day: White
Incense of the Day: Clary sage

Gratitude Meditation

It is always good to take an attitude of gratitude. No matter how difficult things might be, or what you might feel your life is lacking, there are still so many ways in which you are fortunate. It can be helpful to occasionally take the time to remind yourself of all that you have.

Light a white candle in a firesafe container and place it where it can't be knocked over. Then sit or stand comfortably in front of it. Take a few deep breaths and focus on the beauty of the light. Then close your eyes and meditate for a while on the blessings in your life. These may be as simple as food on the table, a cat for company, good weather, or a job you enjoy. Don't forget to be grateful for the very act of breathing. When you are done, blow out the candle with gratitude for its light and warmth.

Deborah Blake

November 23
Tuesday

3rd ♋

Color of the Day: Red
Incense of the Day: Geranium

Journey Spell

When traveling, one of the best stones to take with you on your journey is black tourmaline. It is one of the most widely used stones for grounding and spiritual protection. This stone can also be used to remove negative energies around you.

Before you leave on your travels, place the black tourmaline in your receptive hand (which is usually the left hand if you are right-handed and vice versa). Close your eyes, concentrate on the energy of the stone, and imagine yourself arriving safely at your destination. After you have visualized your safe arrival, place the black tourmaline stone in a small bag that you use for crystals and stones. Keep this bag either on your person, in a pocket, or in a handbag until you arrive back home.

Sapphire Moonbeam

November 24
Wednesday

3rd ♋

☽ v/c 12:46 am

☽ → ♌ 10:59 am

Color of the Day: Yellow
Incense of the Day: Lavender

Spirit Element Meditation

Of all the elements, spirit is the most intangible. To get in touch with the element of spirit, adorn your altar with black and white decorations, white candles, and clear quartz crystals. Sit before your altar in the candlelight and hold a pentacle in your hands. Visualize yourself at the center of the universe, connecting with the energy of all things. You are everywhere and nowhere all at once. Whisper this chant to help with focus if necessary:

Transcend, transcend;
the beginning and the end
will blend. Find the center,
the beginning, and the end—

I enter. Feel the spirit,
above and below, over and under.
Let it fill me with wisdom
and with wonder.

Ember Grant

November 25
Thursday

3rd ♌

Color of the Day: White
Incense of the Day: Nutmeg

Thanksgiving Day

Thank Mother Earth Ritual

The Thanksgiving celebration centers around food, so it seems only right to honor Mother Earth on this holiday. For this ritual of thanks, prepare your menu and set your table as usual. However, be sure to include a dish of corn. Corn is associated with the mother goddess and is one of the most sacred of all foods. You may simply heat up some canned or frozen corn. Place the dish of corn near the head of the table. When everyone is seated, the host/hostess should briefly raise the dish of corn, then say alone or as a group:

Mother Earth, we've scarred
you, but you still give.

Your bounty allows us to live.

With caring hearts and working hands,

We thank your soil found in all lands.

Let us honor you in this small way,

As we give thanks on this
Thanksgiving Day.

Reserve a few kernels of corn. Later, scatter the reserved corn outside on the earth.

James Kambos

November 26
Friday

3rd ♌

☽ v/c 11:24 am

☽ → ♍ 9:12 pm

Color of the Day: Pink

Incense of the Day: Violet

Anti-Black Friday Gratitude Ritual

The holiday season is a wonderful time to enjoy friends and family, but it can be easy to forget that this doesn't have to include overspending, overconsumption, or the stress that can sometimes surround shopping for others. To remind yourself of the blessings you already have and encourage closeness with loved ones, do this ritual, either alone or with a group.

Place a bowl in the middle of the table. Each participant should have a pile of tokens of some kind. You may use marbles, beads, pieces of candy, or practically anything small. Everyone should have at least ten tokens.

Take turns going around and dropping a token in the bowl while expressing gratitude for a blessing in your life. Be as specific as possible. You must take a turn for each token, which may mean that you have to dig a little! A higher number of tokens challenges participants to reach for blessings they might otherwise have forgotten about.

Thorn Mooney

 ## November 27
Saturday

3rd ♍

4th Quarter 7:28 am

Color of the Day: Indigo

Incense of the Day: Magnolia

Knot Magic Manifestation

To manifest something, use knot magic to focus your intent. Take a three-foot-long piece of string or cord. Close your eyes and envision what you want to bring into reality. As you tie each of nine knots, say the phrase below, and in as much detail as possible, see your desires coming to fruition. When the cord is complete, keep it on your altar so it stays in sight and you continue to draw your desires to you.

By knot of one, my magic has begun.

By knot of two, my words ring true.

By knot of three, things come to me.

By knot of four, I create more.

By knot of five, this energy is alive.

By knot of six, this spell is fixed.

By knot of seven, the answer is given.

By knot of eight, I align with fate.

By knot of nine, this thing is mine.

So be it.

Dallas Jennifer Cobb

November 28
Sunday

4th ♏

☽ v/c 7:02 pm

Color of the Day: Gold
Incense of the Day: Frankincense

hanukkah begins at sundown

Witch's homestead Spell

This spell will help enchant your home, making it a sacred place of love, magic, healing, power, and protection. Gather these materials:

- Lavender flowers
- Cinnamon
- Rose petals
- Sea salt
- A large bowl
- 3 pieces of ribbon or yarn: black, red, and green

Ground and center. Using your hands, mix the salt and herbs together in the bowl while saying:

Lavender, cinnamon, rose, and salt,

All baneful spirits you do halt.

Be now filled with health and love,

And draw forth power from above.

Imagine the light of the sun and moon shining down through you to empower this mixture, then sprinkle it around your property to form a barrier and container.

Now take your three pieces of ribbon or yarn and braid them together while chanting:

Ribbons black and red and green,

Bring power from the dark unseen.

Ribbons green and red and black,

Send all unwanted forces back.

Attach this talisman to your front door.

Storm Faerywolf

NOTES:

November 29
Monday

4ᵗʰ ♍︎

☽ → ♎︎ 3:55 am

Color of the Day: Lavender
Incense of the Day: Hyssop

Logic Oil

Mercury recently entered Sagittarius, marking a period of critical thinking and giving us an amazing opportunity to harness the unique energies of the moment to make something that I like to call Logic Oil. Inspired by Star Trek's Spock, this oil is used to inspire people to make the logical, rather than the emotional, choice. To a half-ounce bottle, add the following ingredients:

- 1 pinch dried lavender flower
- 13 drops frankincense essential oil
- 5 drops clove essential oil
- 5 drops tangerine or blood orange essential oil
- 3 drops rue essential oil

Fill the bottle the rest of the way up with a carrier oil, such as fractionated coconut or grapeseed.

Use this oil to dress candles, spell papers, business cards, and other magical items in spellwork when you need people to think with their head and not their heart.

Devin Hunter

 November 30
Tuesday

4ᵗʰ ♎︎

☽ v/c 11:20 pm

Color of the Day: Gray
Incense of the Day: Basil

Secret-Keeping Mirror

Sometimes when we're keeping a secret, it can feel like others will know just by looking at us. This spell is designed to help keep private information hidden. Gather these items:

- A small, inexpensive compact mirror that snaps closed (Even an old, empty makeup one is fine.)
- Black paint
- A paintbrush

Make sure you are all alone and no one is around. Look at your reflection in the little mirror. Hold it close to your mouth and whisper the secret aloud. Snap the compact shut.

Paint the entire outside of the compact black, imagining that the paint is muffling and sealing the contents like a cloak of invisibility. When it is dry, hide it somewhere in your room or house where no one will find it. Leave it there until you no longer need to conceal the secret.

Keep the compact for the next time you have secrets to keep. There's no need to repaint it. Just whisper into the compact and snap it shut.

Kate Freuler

December

December features a palette of cool colors: white snow, silver icicles, evergreen, and, of course, blue—the bright cerulean sky on a clear, cold winter's day, or the deep navy velvet of the darkening nights, culminating on the longest night of the year, the winter solstice. This hue is reflected in December's birthstones: turquoise, zircon, tanzanite, and lapis. The notion of a stone representing each month has been linked to ayurvedic beliefs that suggest correspondences between the planets and crystals. It wasn't until the eighteenth century that associating stones with a birth month became a popular practice in the Western world.

Even if you weren't born in December, you can still tap into the power of this month's special stones. Zircon increases bone stability, which is good for moving over icy terrain. Use turquoise, a rain-making stone, to summon snow. Turquoise also heals and brings peace. Engage tanzanite's powers for psychic visions for the impending new year. Lapis—the mirror of the winter night sky, and a stone that can be found in the breastplate of the high priest—brings wisdom and awareness.

Natalie Zaman

December 1
Wednesday

4th ♎

☽ → ♏ 6:55 am

Color of the Day: Yellow
Incense of the Day: Bay laurel

Eastern Star Spell

Early in the morning, just before the sun rises, the Eastern Star will appear bright in the clear sky and the Queen of the Faeries will hush the world into its winter slumber. Faery dream magick is like pixie dust in a bottle: it's only really useful when it's scattered all about. Leave a trail of all-natural, nonplastic glitter or powdered gemstones across doorways and window ledges to give the Faery Queen a glittering path to enter your home. Leave her sugar cookies and small cups of honeyed milk as a treat, and make your home cozy with extra pillows and blankets so that she will bless the naps and dreams you enjoy this winter. Recite the following prayer.

Prayer to Titania

Swift and pure mist cascades as light.

*A silver bell is ringing to
sweeten her delight.*

*The veil is stretched mithril thin,
glimmers twixt day and night.*

*This morning I summon
Titania into sight.*

Estha McNevin

December 2
Thursday

4th ♏

Color of the Day: Purple
Incense of the Day: Jasmine

Magical Fritters

Today is National Fritters Day in the United States. There is quite a culinary controversy as to what foods are considered fritters, and there are both savory and sweet renditions that are considered contenders for inclusion under the fritter umbrella, including apple fritters, crab cakes, corn fritters, and even Indian pakoras!

Today, take the opportunity to put a magical kitchen witchery spin on this fun day and find a fritter recipe you'd like to make. Tailor the herbs and spices for magical goals. Create fritters for prosperity, good health, happiness, and more! Perhaps organize with a few friends to make different types of fritters—appetizer fritters, entrée fritters, and dessert fritters—then have a magical fritter potluck meal to share the magical properties of all your creations.

Blake Octavian Blair

December 3
Friday

4th ♏

☽ v/c 12:22 am

☽ → ♐ 7:13 am

Color of the Day: Rose
Incense of the Day: Alder

A holly Cleansing Spell

At this time of year, holly is the perfect herb to use to clear away any negative energy in your home. For this spell you'll need a sheet of newspaper, three holly leaves, a piece of stationery, and a pen.

First, lay the sheet of newspaper flat on a table or the floor. Then place the holly leaves in the middle of the newspaper. Write your problem on the stationery. Visualize your problem vanishing. Now tear up the stationery and scatter the pieces over the holly leaves. Wrap the newspaper around the holly leaves and pieces of stationery. Wad it all up and toss it in the trash. Your home will have a more pleasant atmosphere.

James Kambos

NOTES:

December 4
Saturday

4th ♐

New Moon 2:43 am

Color of the Day: Black
Incense of the Day: Rue

Solar Eclipse

Rewrite Your Destiny

A new moon solar eclipse is when the moon moves between the sun and the earth, casting a shadow onto the earth as it blocks the sunlight. If the moon symbolizes spirit, the sun soul, and the earth human life, then an eclipse can represent a new awakening, an opportunity to completely change who we want to be. We can rewrite our own destiny. This eclipse provides energy for transformational change.

Gather paper and pen. Sit quietly. Ask yourself:

What does the world want or need me to be?

Include the expectations of family, work, and society. Write them down on a piece of paper.

On another piece of paper, write:

Who do I need to be?

Shred "what the world wants," saying:

I eclipse others' expectations.

Reread "who you need to be," affirming:

This is exactly, totally, and completely who I get to be.

Each day over the next two weeks, as the moon waxes to full, affirm who you choose to be.

Dallas Jennifer Cobb

December 5
Sunday

1st ♐

☽ v/c 12:08 am

☽ → ♑ 6:31 am

Color of the Day: Yellow

Incense of the Day: Eucalyptus

Self-Esteem Spell

Jupiter has been slowly moving through Aquarius all year and will soon be making its exit. This is the time to plow through issues surrounding your self-esteem and any other personal traits that might make you feel ill-equipped to handle life. Cast this spell to break free from the self-esteem barrier.

You will need the Wheel of Fortune, the Star, and the Empress cards from a tarot deck, as well as a candle of any color. Lay the cards out in the order listed here, ground your energy, and then light the candle.

Touch the Wheel of Fortune card and say:

By Jupiter and fate,
I claim my right!

Then touch the Star card and say:

By Aquarius and hope,
I claim my faith!

Lastly, touch the Empress card and say:

By the Goddess, I claim this life!

By all three, so must it be!

Leave the cards out somewhere visible for thirteen days, and allow the candle to burn out safely on its own.

Devin Hunter

NOTES:

December 6
Monday

1st ♑

☽ v/c 11:42 pm

Color of the Day: Gray
Incense of the Day: Rosemary

Hanukkah ends

Power Nap Spell

For those days when you need to take a quick power nap, use this spell to enhance your slumber and wake up revived and ready to face the rest of your day or night.

Wrap a peppermint leaf (fresh or dried), a piece of sodalite, and a drop or two of lavender essential oil in a bundle and place it in your pillowcase. Chant these words as you visualize the perfect power nap:

For this moment I seize
to catch a few z's,

Make the most of this time
to relax and unwind.

My rest will be blessed,
so I wake up refreshed.

Ember Grant

December 7
Tuesday

1st ♑

☽ → ♒ 6:49 am

Color of the Day: White
Incense of the Day: Bayberry

Mistletoe Spell for Protection and Sweet Dreams

'Tis the season for mistletoe, so this should be relatively easy to obtain. It is a most magical herb that, when hung on the headboard of a bed, has the ability to protect the sleeper not only from danger but from nightmares as well.

To empower the mistletoe with your intention, hold it in both hands and envision it surrounded by pure white light. When you feel the power is at its strongest, say:

Golden bough of magic might,

Grant me this wish to bear.

Protect from harm every night.

Let each sleeper be free of fear.

Hang the mistletoe on the headboard (behind it is fine) of the bed. One of these charms can be made for each bed in your home.

Michael Furie

December 8
Wednesday

1st ♒

Color of the Day: Brown
Incense of the Day: Lilac

To Keep Away Winter Illness

As the autumn holidays come to an end and winter sets in, many of us find ourselves constantly on the verge of sickness. Aside from all of those mundane things we should all be doing to stay healthy (washing hands, getting a flu shot, staying home when we're sick), try this spell to help keep the winter bugs at bay.

Draw a picture of yourself healthy and happy. Don't worry—it doesn't have to be recognizable to anyone else! Just as long as you know it's you. Place it on your altar. With a green or yellow highlighter, draw a circle around yourself in the picture, creating a barrier that shields you from seasonal illness. Say:

I am comfortable, energized, and free from disease. So mote it be.

Then be sure to drink plenty of fluids and wash your hands routinely!

Thorn Mooney

December 9
Thursday

1st ♒

☽ v/c 5:00 am
☽ → ♓ 9:53 am

Color of the Day: Crimson
Incense of the Day: Balsam

Modern Medicine versus Ancient Alternatives

There are times when magical intentions, positive energy, crystals, oils, acupressure, and acupuncture work wonders. Then there are times when only science and medicine will do. Four years ago, I, like countless others before me, faced one of those situations. After several years of pain and trying numerous cures, all of which proved temporary, I had hip replacement surgery. The event was scary but necessary, and it changed my life. My beliefs comforted me during the operation and recovery, and actually brought me closer to my chosen spirit guides. Since that time, I have utilized crystals to keep discomfort at bay and promote continued healing. For anyone struggling with a medical decision, perhaps this verse will help:

Let the healing powers of ancient cures aid my recovery from modern medical processes.

Emyme

 December 10
Friday

1st ♓

2nd Quarter 8:36 pm

Color of the Day: Pink
Incense of the Day: Violet

The Stones of Grounding

Go for a walk in some natural place with the intention of experiencing the earth element, which is associated with structure, stability, and manifestation. It can even be a city park.

On your walk, be aware of any stones, collecting five and bringing them home. Once there, set four of them on the floor in a square, which you will sit inside. Place the other near your root chakra.

Ground and center. Imagine that the life force within the stones is like a green light that dimly shines. As you breathe, imagine these lights slowly reaching out to you in streams of energy that converge in your root and the fifth stone. Say:

Strength of stone

Within my bones.

Put some sea salt on your tongue. Meditate on how you are an extension of the planet. Hold the stones whenever you feel unfocused or in need of grounding.

Storm Faerywolf

 December 11
Saturday

2nd ♓

☽ v/c 2:40 pm

☽ → ♈ 4:46 pm

Color of the Day: Indigo
Incense of the Day: Sandalwood

Empower Yourself

Words have power. You can utilize the power of positive, encouraging words every day. Write words on small pieces of paper and place them in spots around your house where you will notice them. Put the notes on your bathroom mirror, near your desk, and near the doorway. Create notes for yourself that say things like this:

Believe.

Keep going.

I am strong.

I am creative.

I am beautiful.

I am successful.

Create the messages as if you were cheering on your best friend, but extend this love and encouragement to yourself. Using these affirmations daily will help you with strength and empowerment. These magical reminders can assist you in times when you may be struggling and working on overcoming obstacles.

You can do this, you will overcome, you are strong, you will thrive. Believe it.

Sapphire Moonbeam

NOTES:

December 12
Sunday

2nd ♈

Color of the Day: Orange
Incense of the Day: Almond

Crafting Faery Beds

Using recycled materials to craft small beds for the faeries is a fun way to celebrate the Pagan Yuletide and talk about sustainability, recycling, and how to manifest our hopes and dreams for the future in a world where climate change is part of the daily dialogue. Collect milk or juice boxes, soup cans, egg cartons, and other recycled cups or lids that are small enough for a faery to take a nap in. Sculpt and decorate each bed to your liking.

Stuff muslin sachet bags with lavender and dreamtime herbs like chamomile. Craft some cozy blankets by cutting up old shirts and socks. Hang these on a faery altar or keep them around the home to help promote good dreams. Decorate with images of your dreams and aspirations in life, and ask the faeries to dream a little dream of you!

Estha McNevin

December 13
Monday

2nd ♈

☽ v/c 9:52 pm

Color of the Day: Silver
Incense of the Day: Lily

Powerful Number 13

Today is the 13th day of the month. The number thirteen gets a bad rap for many reasons, but for Witches and believers in the occult, the number thirteen is a powerful number. In traditional Witchcraft, it is the number of people in a coven. It is also the usual number of full moons in a year.

As the moon is in its waxing phase right now, let us call forth the power of the coming full moon with this simple charm. You will need a white candle in a fireproof candleholder.

This evening, light your candle and say:

Thirteen Witches gather round,

Singing, chanting, drawing the moon down.

In the night by candlelight,

My hopes, dreams, and wishes take flight.

You can also use this charm when the moon is full.

Najah Lightfoot

 December 14
Tuesday

2nd ♈

☽ → ♉ 3:11 am

Color of the Day: Red
Incense of the Day: Ginger

Clearing Away

Spells often leave some sort of residue behind. This can include candle stubs, incense ash, bits of paper, dried petals, and so on. Most of the time, that gets cleaned up during or after an individual spell. However, sometimes magic happens in haste and not everything gets picked up. Here is a ceremony for clearing away the remnants of old spells.

First take everything off your altar. Empty and wash the incense burner. Empty and clean the candleholders. Polish the athame. Wash the ritual bowls, chalice, and stone or pentacle. Painted icons or other delicate items can simply be dusted. Clean the top of your altar with furniture polish (if wood) or glass cleaner (if glass). Make sure you have a fresh supply of incense, charcoal, candles, and other consumables. Check that the matchbox or lighter is full.

Now place the cleaned altar tools back in their customary positions. Say:

All that has gone before is over and done. What lies ahead is new and clean. So mote it be!

Elizabeth Barrette

NOTES:

December 15
Wednesday

2nd ♉

Color of the Day: White
Incense of the Day: Lavender

Pre-holiday Centering

The holidays are fast approaching. Soon will begin the flurry of family gatherings, grove and coven events, office parties, and potentially visits to churches, temples, or other religious establishments of importance to your family.

Take an opportunity today, before it all sets in, to center yourself in order to put your best foot forward heading into the holiday season. One way to do this comes from druidic traditions, by connecting to land, sky, and sea with three breaths. You can do this anywhere and anytime, so find a quiet spot that works for you. (Fresh outdoor air is a bonus.)

Begin by focusing on the earth below you, and take a deep, slow breath with the earth. Then, focusing on the sky above you, take another deep, slow breath. Then take a third and final deep, slow breath while focusing on the sea that surrounds and connects us.

Blake Octavian Blair

December 16
Thursday

2nd ♉

☽ v/c 11:08 am

☽ → ♊ 3:43 pm

Color of the Day: Turquoise

Incense of the Day: Nutmeg

Decorate Your Altar for Yule

Some Pagans decorate their entire house for Yule, especially if they are living with non-Pagans and combining their Yule celebration with that of Christmas. But if you are someone who doesn't decorate, you may want to at least set up a special Yule altar. You can drape it with pine boughs or a swag made from pine and juniper. Use the colors red, green, and gold, and natural elements like pinecones, acorns, and gourds. You can honor the Goddess in her mother role, since she will give birth to the infant god at Yule, returning the sun to the world. Don't forget that this is a holiday that celebrates the returning light, so if it is safe to do so, be sure to add some candles. (There are some very realistic-looking battery-powered ones available if you can't have flames.) Make your altar cheerful and bright, then spend a few minutes in front of it daily.

Deborah Blake

December 17
Friday

2nd ♊

Color of the Day: Purple

Incense of the Day: Rose

A Pine Blessing

Pine has a purifying quality and is perfect to use in blessing rituals at this time of year. Use this ritual to bless your home and family.

You'll need a bayberry-scented candle, two small pine branches, and a heatproof container, cauldron, or fireplace. Place the candle on your altar and safely light it. In front of the candle, lay the pine branches. Position them so they form a cross. Sit before your altar and say:

Pine, you're an ancient and mighty tree.

Bless my family and our home.

Protect us from any negativity.

End the ritual by burning the pine branches in the heatproof container, cauldron, or fireplace. Snuff out the candle, but continue to burn it as you wish through New Year's Day. When the ashes cool, discard them.

James Kambos

December 18
Saturday

2nd ♊

Full Moon 11:36 pm

Color of the Day: Blue
Incense of the Day: Pine

Protection Cactus

Cacti are available in stores all year round. These tough little potted plants can survive the harshest conditions and are covered in prickles and spikes. This makes them excellent for use as protection or defense charms. Take advantage of this full moon to create a protection cactus for your home. Gather these items:

- 1 teaspoon salt
- A small potted cactus
- Black paint
- A paintbrush

Sprinkle the salt in the shape of a circle onto a surface in front of you. As you do so, say:

Full moon, full protection, full defense.

Imagine that the circle of salt and the moon in the sky are connected by lunar rays.

Using the black paint, draw a protective symbol on the pot, such as a pentacle or the shape of a shield. Place the cactus inside the salt circle. Leave it there overnight to absorb the protective powers of the full moon.

Now you have a protection charm disguised as a cute little cactus! Place it in your home to ward off negative energy. Dispose of the salt.

Kate Freuler

NOTES:

December 19
Sunday

3rd ♊

☽ v/c 1:02 am

☽ → ♋ 4:42 am

Color of the Day: Gold

Incense of the Day: Heliotrope

Sanctuary Spell

The moon is in its home sign of Cancer for most of the day, and we may be feeling a desire to be around a few less people today and stick to ourselves. The winter solstice draws near, and the things that truly matter are likely to be on our mind. Before the rush of the holidays takes full effect, use the power of the Cancer moon to create a place of sanctuary and peace in your home.

For this spell you will need some lavender water and four small to medium-size pieces of citrine, selenite, black tourmaline, or clear quartz. Cleanse your home and the stones using your favorite method, then place one stone each at the front door, back door, common area, and bedroom. Next, lightly sprinkle lavender water around your home and chant the following verse repeatedly until you have covered the entire home:

This sanctuary is blessed by the Goddess; the Goddess resides within this space.

Devin Hunter

 December 20
Monday

3rd ♋

Color of the Day: White

Incense of the Day: Hyssop

Ancient Mysteries

Many of our rituals have origins in ancient traditions, yet when we perform these rites, we connect to something deep within ourselves that defies explanation. Today, concentrate on an old story or myth that calls to you.

For this spell you will need a black candle, frankincense essential oil, gold glitter, a fireproof candleholder, a pen, and paper.

Anoint your candle with frankincense oil, then roll it in gold glitter. Place it in the holder.

Light the candle. As you gaze into the flame, say:

Ancient mysteries of old,

By this divine light you unfold.

By dark of night, by light of day,

I thank you for all you share with me today.

Write down any impressions you receive, then extinguish the candle or let it burn down safely. Keep the paper and candle on your altar as a reminder of your connection to the divine mysteries.

Najah Lightfoot

 December 21
Tuesday

3rd ♋

☽ v/c *9:44 am*

☉ → ♑ *10:59 am*

☽ → ♌ *4:54 pm*

Color of the Day: Maroon

Incense of the Day: Ylang-ylang

Yule — Winter Solstice

Yuletide Peace Brew

Yule is traditionally associated with family gatherings, gift giv-ing, and holiday parties, and this quick bit of magical cookery can help ensure that the home environment will remain happy and peaceful for all to enjoy. This brew can be simmered on the stove to release a peaceful and loving energy as well as a comforting warmth. Gather these ingredients:

- 1 cup water
- 1 cup apple juice
- 3 cinnamon sticks, broken
- 1 tablespoon pumpkin pie spice
- 1 tablespoon vanilla extract
- 1 tablespoon almond extract
- 1 orange, sliced

Combine all the ingredients in a caul-dron or pot and simmer on low for as long as desired, adding more water if necessary.

Michael Furie

▽ **December 22**
Wednesday

3rd ♌

Color of the Day: Topaz

Incense of the Day: Honeysuckle

Attune with Earth

Now that the solstice has passed and winter has officially arrived, the daylight hours will very gradually increase, with the promise of spring to someday arrive (however far away). But first we must pass through win-ter! In many Western magical tradi-tions, winter is tied to the north and the element of earth, which rules over groundedness, stability, the physical body, and silence. To get the most out of the coming months, attune to the element of earth.

If you can, sit on the earth outside, perhaps under a tree. If you must remain indoors, you may do this with a pot of earth or a bowl of salt. Place your hands in the soil or salt and con-template the stillness of the season. Root your own energy here, feeling the connection in your bones. Say:

Powers of the earth, lend me your
gifts of strength, stability, and the
power to remain silent. Be with
me this day. So mote it be.

Thorn Mooney

December 23
Thursday

3rd ♌

Color of the Day: Green
Incense of the Day: Myrrh

Larentalia

This day was dedicated to a Roman goddess (possibly named Larentia or Lara) who was said to be the guardian of ghosts—specifically the *Lares*, or good spirits. Offerings were made to her on this day for the departed spirits. These spirits were believed to be the protectors of homes and families. The offerings were typically left in chimney corners, where the Lares were said to dwell.

On this day, leave your own offering for the protection of your home and family. Place the offering near a chimney or hearth, if you have one. If not, any corner of the home will do. Offer a small piece of bread or some dried beans or lentils. Leave the items in place for at least twenty-four hours, then put them outside. Each time you put the offering in place, say these words:

Keep us all from harm,

Protect and guard this home.

Grant us safety while we're here

And also when we roam.

Ember Grant

December 24
Friday

3rd ♌

☽ v/c 1:39 am
☽ → ♍ 3:24 am

Color of the Day: Coral
Incense of the Day: Mint

Christmas Eve

A Merry Witchy Christmas Spell

Christmas is more than just a religious celebration. It's also a secular celebration of family and abundance in wintertime, and of Santa Claus, an old man who flies through the sky with eight magical reindeer and some elves. It's Pagan through and through.

For this spell you will need the following items:

• A small gift
• Wrapping paper and ribbon
• Scissors
• Tape
• 2 candy canes

Wrap your gift while playing or singing a Christmas song. Eat one candy cane and affix the other to the wrapped package. As you tie the bow, say:

Tonight he rides the winter sky,

To bring the gifts of light and hope.

Choose a person at random and give them the gift anonymously. Santa Claus is alive and well. Merry Christmas!

Storm Faerywolf

Notes:

December 25
Saturday

3rd ♍

Color of the Day: Gray
Incense of the Day: Sage

Christmas Day

holiday Balance

Depending on your lifestyle, Saturday may just be the perfect day of the week to celebrate Christmas. This is the time of year for parties and get-togethers with family, friends, coworkers, and spiritual groups.

With all these celebrations, be aware of potential holiday burnout. Today, take some time (five minutes will do) to find a quiet place and concentrate on peace and well-being for all people in the world. Send out positive energy for safe travel. Create a blessing for all those workers who sacrifice their time to make life better for others at the holidays. Take a deep, calming inhale and exhale, give thanks to the Lady and Lord, and begin your day feeling refreshed. Here is a suggested mantra:

Joy is mine—I share it.

Love is mine—I share it.

May this day find all safe, heathy, and whole.

All is well. Life is good.

Emyme

December 26
Sunday

3rd ♍

☽ v/c 3:39 am

☽ → ♎ 11:24 am

4th Quarter 9:24 pm

Color of the Day: Amber
Incense of the Day: Marigold

Kwanzaa begins –
Boxing Day (Canada & UK)

Gifts to Ourselves

In the Victorian era, Boxing Day was traditionally the only day servants had off from work, and they often received a boxed gift from their master or mistress.

A statutory holiday here in Canada, Boxing Day is a time for me to focus on giving to myself and being my own "mistress." I give myself a small magical gift wrapped up in a box.

Today, cast a circle, call in the directions, and invoke Mother Mary, a symbol of the divine feminine. May she connect you to your own divinity. While in sacred space, imagine being held in Mother Mary's arms, by the divine feminine, protected and empowered. Open the box and joyously

receive the magical gift, affirming:

I am my own mistress, thankful for my own divine care. I receive this gift and empower the magic of my divine feminine. I give and receive magic.

Close the circle. Create a magical life.

Dallas Jennifer Cobb

Notes:

December 27
Monday

4℞ ♎

Color of the Day: Ivory
Incense of the Day: Neroli

Dreamtime Tea

There is nothing quite so nourishing as a good night's sleep full of deep and safe dreams. This tea is crafted to be safe and effective for children and is a good part of the bedtime routine because it calms the stomach, flushes the system, and warms the body before bed. It inspires vivid dreams that encourage deep REM sleep and help us wake feeling more fully rested. A little goes a long way, because the fruity flavor is refreshing.

This recipe makes 2½ cups of dry herbal tea, which can fill a hundred bags with one teaspoon each. Enchant the mixture with prayers for sound and visionary sleep.

- ½ cup dehydrated raspberries, crushed
- ¼ cup chamomile
- ¼ cup tulsi (holy basil)
- ¼ cup peppermint
- ¼ cup mugwort
- ½ cup rose hips
- 1 cup dehydrated blueberries, crushed

Estha McNevin

December 28

Tuesday

4th ♎

☽ v/c 4:11 pm

☽ → ♏ 4:16 pm

Color of the Day: Scarlet
Incense of the Day: Cedar

Food of the Gods

Today is National Chocolate Candy Day. Chocolate is one of the most popular types of candy and is also an entheogen, which opens one's soul to the divine. You may have heard it personified as the goddess Chocolata. The Mayan goddess of chocolate is Ixcacao, and the Aztec one is Xochiquetzal. You can invoke any of them for this ritual.

Get a bag of chocolate coins covered in gold foil, which are readily available this time of year as Hanukkah gelt or stocking stuffers. Place the coins in a brown bowl on your altar. Then say:

Chocolate, food of the gods,
fill my life with sweetness.

Gold, metal of wealth, coat
my life with prosperity.

Chocolata, goddess of chocolate,
open my soul to your abundance.

So mote it be!

Eat one of the coins now, savoring its sweetness. Whenever you need a boost to your abundance, eat another one, for as long as they last.

Elizabeth Barrette

NOTES:

December 29
Wednesday

4th ♏

Color of the Day: Yellow
Incense of the Day: Marjoram

heart and Soul Balance Spell

As we approach the end of the calendar year, it is a perfect time to work on balance. Life has many ups and downs, and finding balance can sometimes be challenging. Sometimes our balance is thrown off by fear.

When you need to regain balance and harmony, draw a yin-yang symbol on a piece of paper. Place the paper on your altar or sacred space, then put quartz crystals on top of the lines of the drawing. The quartz crystals will amplify your intention to find balance. Take three deep breaths to ground and center yourself. Continue the deep breathing until you feel peaceful and calm. Then, when you are ready, chant these words:

I release my struggle,
I surrender my fear.

I will maintain balance,
My intentions are clear.

I will focus on balance
with my heart aglow.

My soul will center with
an effortless flow.

Sapphire Moonbeam

 December 30
Thursday

4th ♏
☽ v/c 12:10 pm
☽ → ♐ 6:08 pm

Color of the Day: White
Incense of the Day: Clove

Prepare Your Altar for a New Year

Some people leave their Yule altars up for a while after the holiday, but it can be nice to start the new year fresh. The altar is a good place to start to clear away the energy of the year behind you and open yourself to the possibilities a new year holds.

Begin by taking everything off your altar. Clean and dust the altar itself, and anything that will be going back onto it. As you arrange items back on the altar, be mindful of what you want to achieve in the year to come. If you want love, perhaps add a heart-shaped rock or a dried rose. If prosperity is your goal, try placing a shiny dollar coin near a green candle. Move things around until it feels balanced and positive, then say:

God and Goddess, please bless
this new altar, prepared for a new
year. May it serve my magic well.

Deborah Blake

 December 31
Friday

4♌ ♐

Color of the Day: Pink
Incense of the Day: Orchid

New Year's Eve

New Year's Eve Banishing Salt

To make this banishing salt, you will need one tablespoon sea or table salt and three drops tea tree oil, plus an envelope or other container.

On New Year's Eve, take a quiet moment to yourself during the festivities. Hold the salt in the palm of your hand and think about something from the past year that you'd like to let go of. This can be many things or only one thing. Whisper your wish to the salt, allowing your breath to get onto it, imbuing it with your intention. Then add the tea tree oil to the salt. Place it in the envelope or container.

At midnight if possible, toss your salt away from you into the wind outdoors, or wash it down the drain. (This can be done discreetly if you're around other people.) See the old year wash away from you, and welcome the new calendar year with a clear sense of hope. Recycle or reuse the envelope or container.

Kate Freuler

Daily Magical Influences

Each day is ruled by a planet that possesses specific magical influences:

Monday (Moon): peace, healing, caring, psychic awareness, purification.

Tuesday (Mars): passion, sex, courage, aggression, protection.

Wednesday (Mercury): conscious mind, study, travel, divination, wisdom.

Thursday (Jupiter): expansion, money, prosperity, generosity.

Friday (Venus): love, friendship, reconciliation, beauty.

Saturday (Saturn): longevity, exorcism, endings, homes, houses.

Sunday (Sun): healing, spirituality, success, strength, protection.

Lunar Phases

The lunar phase is important in determining best times for magic.

The waxing moon (from the new moon to the full moon) is the ideal time for magic to draw things toward you.

The full moon is the time of greatest power.

The waning moon (from the full moon to the new moon) is a time for study, meditation, and little magical work (except magic designed to banish harmful energies).

Astrological Symbols

The Sun	☉	Aries	♈
The Moon	☽	Taurus	♉
Mercury	☿	Gemini	♊
Venus	♀	Cancer	♋
Mars	♂	Leo	♌
Jupiter	♃	Virgo	♍
Saturn	♄	Libra	♎
Uranus	♅	Scorpio	♏
Neptune	♆	Sagittarius	♐
Pluto	♇	Capricorn	♑
		Aquarius	♒
		Pisces	♓

The Moon's Sign

The moon's sign is a traditional consideration for astrologers. The moon continuously moves through each sign in the zodiac, from Aries to Pisces. The moon influences the sign it inhabits, creating different energies that affect our daily lives.

Aries: Good for starting things but lacks staying power. Things occur rapidly but quickly pass. People tend to be argumentative and assertive.

Taurus: Things begun now do last, tend to increase in value, and become hard to alter. Brings out an appreciation for beauty and sensory experience.

Gemini: Things begun now are easily changed by outside influence. Time for shortcuts, communications, games, and fun.

Cancer: Stimulates emotional rapport between people. Pinpoints need, supports growth and nurturance. Tend to domestic concerns.

Leo: Draws emphasis to the self, to central ideas or institutions, away from connections with others and emotional needs. People tend to be melodramatic.

Virgo: Favors accomplishment of details and commands from higher up. Focus on health, hygiene, and daily schedules.

Libra: Favors cooperation, compromise, social activities, beautification of surroundings, balance, and partnership.

Scorpio: Increases awareness of psychic power. Favors activities requiring intensity and focus. People tend to brood and become secretive under this moon sign.

Sagittarius: Encourages flights of imagination and confidence. This moon sign is adventurous, philosophical, and athletic. Favors expansion and growth.

Capricorn: Develops strong structure. Focus on traditions, responsibilities, and obligations. A good time to set boundaries and rules.

Aquarius: Rebellious energy. Time to break habits and make abrupt change. Personal freedom and individuality are the focus.

Pisces: The focus is on dreaming, nostalgia, intuition, and psychic impressions. A good time for spiritual or philanthropic activities.

Glossary of Magical Terms

Altar: A table that holds magical tools as a focus for spell workings.

Athame: A ritual knife used to direct personal power during workings or to symbolically draw diagrams in a spell. It is rarely, if ever, used for actual physical cutting.

Aura: An invisible energy field surrounding a person. The aura can change color depending on the state of the individual.

Balefire: A fire lit for magical purposes, usually outdoors.

Casting a circle: The process of drawing a circle around oneself to seal out unfriendly influences and raise magical power. It is the first step in a spell.

Censer: An incense burner. Traditionally a censer is a metal container, filled with incense, that is swung on the end of a chain.

Censing: The process of burning incense to spiritually cleanse an object.

Centering yourself: To prepare for a magical rite by calming and centering all of your personal energy.

Chakra: One of the seven centers of spiritual energy in the human body, according to the philosophy of yoga.

Charging: To infuse an object with magical power.

Circle of protection: A circle cast to protect oneself from unfriendly influences.

Crystals: Quartz or other stones that store cleansing or protective energies.

Deosil: Clockwise movement, symbolic of life and positive energies.

Deva: A divine being according to Hindu beliefs; a devil or evil spirit according to Zoroastrianism.

Direct/retrograde: Refers to the motion of a planet when seen from the earth. A planet is "direct" when it appears to be moving forward from the point of view of a person on the earth. It is "retrograde" when it appears to be moving backward.

Dowsing: To use a divining rod to search for a thing, usually water or minerals.

Dowsing pendulum: A long cord with a coin or gem at one end. The pattern of its swing is used to answer questions.

Dryad: A tree spirit or forest guardian.

Fey: An archaic term for a magical spirit or a fairylike being.

Gris-gris: A small bag containing charms, herbs, stones, and other items to draw energy, luck, love, or prosperity to the wearer.

Mantra: A sacred chant used in Hindu tradition to embody the divinity invoked; it is said to possess deep magical power.

Needfire: A ceremonial fire kindled at dawn on major Wiccan holidays. It was traditionally used to light all other household fires.

Pentagram: A symbolically protective five-pointed star with one point upward.

Power hand: The dominant hand; the hand used most often.

Scry: To predict the future by gazing at or into an object such as a crystal ball or pool of water.

Second sight: The psychic power or ability to foresee the future.

Sigil: A personal seal or symbol.

Smudge/smudge stick: To spiritually cleanse an object by waving smoke over and around it. A smudge stick is a bundle of several incense sticks.

Wand: A stick or rod used for casting circles and as a focus for magical power.

Widdershins: Counterclockwise movement, symbolic of negative magical purposes, sometimes used to disperse negative energies.

About the Authors

Elizabeth Barrette has been involved with the Pagan community for more than thirty years. She served as managing editor of *PanGaia* for eight years and dean of studies at the Grey School of Wizardry for four years. She has written columns on beginning and intermediate Pagan practice, Pagan culture, and Pagan leadership. Her book *Composing Magic: How to Create Magical Spells, Rituals, Blessings, Chants, and Prayers* explains how to combine writing and spirituality. She lives in central Illinois, where she has done much networking with Pagans in her area, such as coffeehouse meetings and open sabbats. Her other public activities include Pagan picnics and science fiction conventions. She enjoys magical crafts, historical religions, and gardening for wildlife. Her other writing fields include speculative fiction, gender studies, and social and environmental issues. Visit her blog, *The Wordsmith's Forge* (https://ysabetwordsmith.dreamwidth.org/), or website, *PenUltimate Productions* (http://penultimateproductions.weebly.com). Her coven site, with extensive Pagan materials, is *Greenhaven Tradition* (http://greenhaventradition.weebly.com/).

Blake Octavian Blair is a shamanic practitioner, ordained minister, writer, Usui Reiki Master-Teacher, tarot reader, and musical artist. He incorporates mystical traditions from both the East and the West with a reverence for the natural world into his own brand of spirituality. He holds a degree in English and religion from the University of Florida. He is an avid reader, knitter, and crafter, and a member of the Order of Bards, Ovates & Druids. Blake loves communing with nature and exploring its beauty. He lives in the New England region of the US with his beloved husband. Visit him on the web at www.blakeoctavianblair.com or write him at blake@blakeoctavianblair.com.

Deborah Blake is the award-winning author of twelve books on modern Witchcraft, including *The Little Book of Cat Magic, The Goddess Is in the Details, Everyday Witchcraft*, and numerous other books from Llewellyn, along with the Everyday Witch tarot and oracle decks. She has published many articles in the Llewellyn annuals, and her ongoing column, "Everyday Witchcraft," is featured in *Witches & Pagans* magazine. She has also written the Baba Yaga and Broken Rider paranormal romance series and the Veiled Magic urban fantasies from Berkley. When not writing, Deborah runs the Artisans' Guild, a cooperative shop she founded with a friend in

1999, and also works as a jewelry maker, tarot reader, and energy healer. She lives in a 130-year-old farmhouse in rural upstate New York with multiple cats who supervise all her activities, both magical and mundane. She can be found online at www.deborahblakeauthor.com.

Dallas Jennifer Cobb lives in a magical village on Lake Ontario. A Pagan, mother, feminist, writer, and animal lover, she has conjured a sustainable lifestyle with a balance of time and money. Widely published, she writes about what she knows: brain injury, magick, herbs, astrology, abundance, recovery, and vibrant sustainability. When she isn't communing with nature, she likes to correspond with like-minded beings. Reach her at jennifer.cobb@live.com.

Emyme has been writing for many years, and those years have brought some changes. Her daughter, one perfect Rose, has given her a granddaughter, the beloved Aurora. This places Emyme firmly and happily in crone status. One cat continues to garner all the rest of her love. Retirement looms on the horizon, which will finally provide her with more time to write. All is well. Life is good. Contact Emyme at Catsmeow24@verizon.net.

Storm Faerywolf is a professional author, teacher, warlock, priest, and initiate of the Faery tradition, where he holds the Black Wand of a Master. He is the author of several books, including *Betwixt and Between* and *Forbidden Mysteries of Faery Witchcraft*. He is a regular contributor to both ModernWitch.com and The Wild Hunt and is one of the founders of the Black Rose school of witchcraft. He makes his home with his loving partners in the San Francisco Bay and travels internationally teaching the magical arts. For more, visit his website at Faerywolf.com.

Kate Freuler lives in Ontario, Canada, and is the author of *Of Blood and Bones: Working with Shadow Magick & the Dark Moon*. She has owned and operated the witchcraft shop www.whitemoonwitchcraft.com for ten years. When she's not writing or crafting items for clients, she is busy being creative with art or reading a huge stack of books.

Michael Furie (Northern California) is the author of *Supermarket Sabbats, Spellcasting for Beginners, Supermarket Magic, Spellcasting: Beyond the Basics*, and more, all from Llewellyn. A practicing Witch for more than twenty years, he is a priest of the Cailleach. He can be found online at www.michaelfurie.com.

Ember Grant has been writing for the Llewellyn annuals for more than fifteen years and is the author of three books. She lives in Missouri with her husband of twenty-five years and two very spoiled feline companions.

Devin Hunter (San Francisco Bay Area) is a bestselling author who holds initiations in multiple spiritual, occult, and esoteric traditions and is the founder of his own tradition, Sacred Fires, and cofounder of its offshoot community, Black Rose Witchcraft. His podcast, *The Modern Witch*, has helped thousands of people from all over the world empower themselves and discover their psychic and magical abilities. Devin is the co-owner of the Mystic Dream, a metaphysical store in Walnut Creek, CA, where he offers professional services as a medium and occultist.

James Kambos became interested in spells and folk magic after watching his grandmother cast spells based on her Greek heritage. He writes and paints from his home in the Appalachian hill country of Southern Ohio.

Najah Lightfoot is the author of *Good Juju: Mojos, Rites & Practices for the Magical Soul*, published by Llewellyn. She is an initiated member of La Source Ancienne Ounfo, a private Vodou society in New Orleans, as well as a sister-priestess of the Divine Feminine and an active member of the Denver Pagan community. She keeps her magick strong through the practice of kung fu, the folk magick of Hoodoo, Pagan rituals, and her belief in the mysteries of the universe. She finds inspiration in movies, music, and the blue skies of Colorado. Najah is a regular contributing author to the Llewellyn annuals and a frequent guest on podcasts. She is also a frequent contributor to many online sites, including InStyle.com, VoyageDenver.com, and NewOrleansHealingCenter.org. She can be found online at www.twitter .com/NajahLightfoot, www.facebook.com/NajahLightfoot, and www.instagram .com/NajahLightfoot.

Estha McNevin (Missoula, MT) is a Priestess and Eastern Hellenistic oracle of Opus Aima Obscuræ, a nonprofit matriarchal Pagan temple haus. Since 2003 she has dedicated her life to working as a ceremonialist, psychic, lecturer, freelance author, and artist. In addition to hosting public sabbats, Estha organizes annual philanthropic projects, teaches classes, counsels clients, manages the temple farm, conducts ceremonies, and officiates for the temple divination rituals each dark moon. To learn more, please explore www.opusaimaobscurae.org and www.facebook.com/opusaimaobscurae.

Sapphire Moonbeam is a rainbow-inspired energy artist, metaphysical jewelry maker, and nature photographer, as well as a crystal, flower, fairy, and tree lover. She is the artist and author of the Moonbeam Magick oracle card deck. Sapphire teaches intuitive abstract art classes in the Kansas City area, and also teaches at locations around the world. She travels with women's spiritual retreats and connects with the mystical energies at ancient sites in Egypt, Greece, India, Peru, Scotland, Turkey, and more. She has a world-wide following at her Sapphire's Moonbeams page on Facebook. Visit her website at SapphireMoonbeam.com.

Thorn Mooney is the author of *Traditional Wicca: A Seeker's Guide*. A Wiccan priestess and coven leader in the Gardnerian tradition, Thorn has been practicing witchcraft since the late nineties. She has been blogging, making YouTube videos, and producing other magical online content for more than a decade. Find her on Instagram @thornthewitch and visit her at www.thornthewitch.com. Thorn lives in North Carolina, where she works in publishing and remains active in local communities.

Spell Notes

Spell Notes

Spell Notes